A FUTURE FULL OF HOPE?

I know the plans I have in mind for you – it is the Lord who speaks –
plans for peace, not disaster, reserving a future full of hope for you.
Jeremiah 29:11

Gemma Simmonds CJ

A Future Full of Hope?

Foreword by

Timothy Radcliffe, OP

LITURGICAL PRESS

Collegeville, Minnesota

www.litpress.org

Published in 2013 for the United States and Canada by
Liturgical Press
Collegeville, Minnesota 56321

First published in 2012 by The Columba Press, Blackrock, Co. Dublin.

Cover by Bill Bolger
Origination by The Columba Press

Library of Congress Control Number: 2013939524

ISBN 978-0-8146-3802-6
ISBN 978-0-8146-3827-9 (e-book)

Contents

Foreword by Timothy Radcliffe OP   7

Acknowledgments   11

Contributors   13

Introduction   15

PART ONE: RELIGIOUS LIFE – FUNDAMENTAL QUESTIONS

1   Giving Religious Life a Theology Transfusion   23
Gregory Collins OSB

2   The Complexities and Difficulties of a Return *ad fontes*   38
Mary Finbarr Coffey HC

3   Sustaining Presence:
Religious Life in the Midst of Creation   52
Martin Poulsom SDB

4   'Nothing was taken from me: everything was given':
Religious Life and Second Wave Feminism   63
Kate Stogdon RC

PART TWO: THE ONCE AND FUTURE VOCATION

5   Compass in the Catholic Church:
Finding a Path to Vocation Discernment   80
Christopher Jamison OSB

6   Young People in Search of Religious Vocation   92
Joanna Gilbert

7   The Dominicans and Vocations   106
Gerard Dunne OP

PART THREE: FORWARD INTO THE FUTURE

8   Religious Life: A Question of Visibility   116
Gemma Simmonds CJ

9   Religious Life Looks to its Future   129
James Sweeney CP

Bibliography   145

Foreword

Timothy Radcliffe OP

This is a wonderful moment for this new book on religious life, because it prepares us for its imminent revival in the West. Religious life is flourishing in other parts of the world, especially Asia and Africa, but in recent decades vocations have been few in America and Western Europe. But a revival is due here too. Indeed, as this book shows, there are already signs that it has begun.

Why I am so hopeful? Because this is a time of crisis and, as I have often insisted, the church is renewed through crisis. The story of salvation is about crises which lead to renaissance. The fall, the flood, repeated exile and the destruction of God's holy temple all led us closer to sharing in God's life in Jesus. Every Sunday we remember the worst crisis of all, the Last Supper, when it became clear that the disciples would lose Jesus, that they would deny him, run away and that their fragile little community would collapse. And in this darkest moment, when all seemed lost, then he gave them himself more intimately than ever before: 'This is my body given for you'. So crises are not to be feared. My American brethren gave me a T-shirt which said, 'Have a good crisis.' Unfortunately it has shrunk during the years and I can no longer get into it.

God comes to us in crises because that is how human beings flourish. We grow by one crisis after another: birth, weaning, adolescence, leaving home, and ultimately death. Each is a crisis that may move us into deeper intimacy with each other and with God. So this difficult time for religious life will surely also ultimately be a blessing and lead to renewal, perhaps in ways that we cannot anticipate.

But this will only happen if we are not obsessed with our own survival. Why should anyone join us so that we may survive? Survival is not a Christian value. Jesus did not say, 'I have come that you may survive' but 'so that you may have life and have it abundantly.' We need to be turned outwards, liberated from excessive self-preoccupation, and be attentive to the needs of our church and our world. That implies a sort of death and resurrection.

The desert fathers and mothers responded to the crisis of the church after the conversion of Constantine when bishops became lords and the poor were forgotten. Religious life began because the church seemed to be slipping into compromise. St Benedict responded to the crisis of the end of the Latin Roman Empire, and the establishment of the Gothic Arian Kings when Catholic civilisation seemed finished. The mendicant friars arose in the thirteenth century because the church was out of touch with the new life and vitality of the cities and the universities. The crisis of the Reformation and the new individualism of the Renaissance led to the foundation of the Jesuits, the Ursulines and the Capuchins and profound renewal of the church. The crisis of the Industrial Revolution and new urban poverty and suffering saw the birth of most of today's religious congregations. Nearly all our orders and congregations were born in response to crises of society or of the church.

So if we wish to grasp this potentially fruitful moment and flourish, then we must ask what are the crises that shake our people. How do they hurt? How can we be with them now? If we respond with courage, then we shall have a future. If we try to recruit new members just to survive, then we shall not deserve to do so. I am sometimes amused when religious tell me that they are opening a new presence in the Philippines as part of their mission, in a country which has one of the highest levels of Catholic practice in the world.

Ever since the conversion of Constantine, religious life has been a vital part of the life of the church. At times we religious have been tempted to think that this was because of the superiority of our vocation. In recent decades we have learned more humility and discovered the equal beauty of the vocation of all the baptised. Sometimes this has been experienced as an undermining of our vocation. What is the point of embracing our strange way of life, with its vows of poverty, chastity and obedience, if it is no better way to holiness than settling down to marriage?

But the beauty of religious life does not lie in any spurious claim to superiority but because it is a stark expression of the extraordinary vocation of every human being, which is to respond to the call to share God's life, joy and freedom. In the Old Testament God bursts into the lives of Abraham, Moses and the prophets by calling them by name, to which they respond: 'Here I am.' Every human being is called into existence and is invited to make the same response. When we make our vows, and promise obedience to God and to our congregations, then we are making a naked expression of the drama of every human being. What is wonderful about religious life is that it expresses the glorious destiny of being human.

For the first one and a half thousand years of Christianity all Christians believed that baptism engaged us in the most wonderful and terrifying adventure. We are being taken up in Christ into the very Godhead. As the early fathers said: 'God became human so that humans might become divine.' Leo the Great, the fifth-century pope, said in his wonderful sermon for Christmas Day: 'Christian, remember your dignity, now that you share in God's own nature.' Human beings are made for more than merely human flourishing. It belongs to our nature to find fulfilment in nothing less than life in the Trinity. This was a bold vision which undergirds the startling excess of our Christian ancestors, and was expressed in radical generosity, in heroic virtue and in the flourishing from the fourth century onwards of religious life.

Charles Taylor links the birth of secularism with the loss of this sense of adventure. After the seventeenth century, it comes to be accepted that it is enough to be human: 'A secular age is one in which the eclipse of all goals beyond human flourishing becomes conceivable.'[1] Christianity is domesticated, and eternal bliss is seen as a sort of retirement to the celestial equivalent of Brighton.

Once Christianity loses that promise of utter transformation, indeed divinisation, then religious life came to be seen as unnecessary and even inhuman: 'If God's purpose for us is simply that we flourish, and we flourish by the judicious use of industry and instrumental reason, then what possible use could he have for a Saint Francis, who in a great élan of love calls on his followers

---

1. Charles Taylor, *A Secular Age*, Harvard University Press, 2007, p.19

to dedicate themselves to a life of poverty. At best, this must lower GNP, by withdrawing these mendicants from the workforce; but worse, it can lower the morale of the productive. Better to accept the limitations of our nature as self-loving creatures, and make the best of it'.[2]

If Christianity is to flourish in the West, then we must recapture a sense of the profound adventure of our faith. Young people do not want a religion which offers a just vague, warm spirituality, a lifestyle accessory like aromatherapy or a fitness regime. Their imagination will be touched if we embody the staggering invitation to share God's own life. Religious life will surely revive in our time, precisely because its craziness points to God's unimaginable promise to us all.

2. Ibid, p.230

Acknowledgements

This book is a collection of papers given at a colloquium on the future of religious life held at Worth Abbey, Sussex, in April 2010. The colloquium itself was the brainchild of the Steering Committee of the Religious Life Institute, based at Heythrop College. Much discussion and hard work went into it before the idea became an event, and much is owed to the insight and energy of: Ann Cunningham (Newcastle Dominicans), Benedict Foy (De la Salle Brothers), Damian Howard (Jesuits, Heythrop College), Christopher Jamison (Benedictines), Cath Lloyd (Religious of the Sacred Heart), Margaret O'Shea (Poor Servants of the Mother of God), Martin Poulsom (Salesians of Don Bosco, Heythrop College), Catherine Skelton (Daughters of St Paul), Kate Stogdon (Cenacle) and Paul Rout (Franciscans, Heythrop College) and to the energy and persistence of Sister Maureen Connor (Religious of the Assumption) who was project manager of the Religious Life Institute 2008-2010 and did sterling work preparing for and organising the event itself, when she had the assistance of Lotte Webb of the Compass Group. A colloquium, like an army, marches on its stomach and needs to be housed in a place conducive to thought and reflective discussion. Our thanks to Abbot Christopher Jamison OSB and the community at Worth, who gave us house room, and especially to Fr Patrick Fludder OSB, who was such a welcoming guestmaster.

In addition to the contributors to this book there were other participants whose enthusiastic and searching insights, questions and comments made a significant difference to the final outcome of the colloquium itself and the revised papers that make up this book. Thanks to: Simon Bishop SJ, Maureen Connor RA, Sarah Dobson CJ, Kitty Ellard IJS, Jackie Gleeson IBVM, Anne Griffiths OSU (now also a member of the RLI Steering Committee), Cathy Jones RA, Margaret O'Shea PSMG, Catherine Skelton FSP and Lotte Webb (Compass Group).

Gerard Dunne OP's paper was read *in absentia*, but discussed in the same way as those of authors present.

A colloquium does not happen without money, and the Religious Life Institute has received generous financial support since its inception from the Conference of Religious of England and Wales. It would also never have been able to establish itself and flourish without the warm support, both moral and practical, of Heythrop College, University of London, its former principal John McDade SJ and current principal Michael Holman SJ.

Finally the urging to produce this book has come from religious all over the UK and Ireland, especially those whom I have met in the course of my many journeys to speak to the Conference of Religious of Ireland and to particular religious congregations within its membership, and that of the Conference of Religious of England and Wales. Ideas, questions and challenges have also come from the religious (and a few lay people) who have attended the Theology of Religious Life module at Heythrop College and religious in Africa, Australia, Mauritius, the United States and across Europe with whom I have engaged in groups and general or provincial chapters. Religious life has taken a battering of recent years, but the best of it is by no means dead yet. The life, energy, dedication, solidarity and generous fidelity among women religious in particular have been an abiding inspiration behind this work.

Gemma Simmonds CJ
Director, Religious Life Institute

Contributors

GREGORY COLLINS OSB is a Benedictine monk and Abbot of the Dormition Abbey in Jerusalem. His latest book is *Meeting Christ in His Mysteries: a Benedictine Vision of the Spiritual Life* (Dublin: Columba Press, 2011).

MARY FINBARR COFFEY HC is a member of the Congregation of the Sisters of the Holy Cross, Menzingen, Switzerland. She lectures in metaphysics and pastoral theology at St John's Seminary, Wonersh, England.

GERARD DUNNE OP is a member of the Irish Dominican province, where he has been the vocations director since 2000.

CHRISTOPHER JAMISON OSB is a Benedictine monk and former Abbot of Worth Abbey. Known to many through his media appearances and his books *Finding Sanctuary and Finding Happiness*, he is currently Director of the National Office for Vocation of the Catholic Church in England and Wales.

JOANNA GILBERT is a member of The Wellspring Community – a newly-formed Benedictine community in Brighton, with members in different states of life. She works in church ministry, particularly with young adults.

MARTIN POULSOM SDB is a Salesian priest. He is a lecturer in Theology at Heythrop College, University of London, and is on the staff of the Religious Life Institute and the Philosophy of Religion Centre there. He is chair of livesimply in the UK and is currently undertaking research in theology of creation.

GEMMA SIMMONDS CJ is a sister of the Congregation of Jesus. She is Director of the Religious Life Institute and a lecturer in pastoral theology at Heythrop College, University of London.

KATE STOGDON RC is a Cenacle sister, who lectures in Christian Spirituality and teaches on the Theology of Religious Life course run by the Religious Life Institute. She is a practising spiritual director.

JAMES SWEENEY CP is a priest of the Passionist Congregation. He is Director of the Heythrop Institute: Religion and Society and senior lecturer in pastoral theology at Heythrop College, University of London.

Introduction

Gemma Simmonds CJ

If it is undoubtedly true that religious life in what is loosely called the West, the developed world or, to move from socio-geographical descriptors to a temporal one, the postmodern era, is in crisis, this is not to say that all forms and manifestations of religious life will disappear. As some orders die, others are in the process of being born. It has ever been thus in the church, and this is a sign both of the vigour of emergent charisms and the effectiveness of established ones. The Spirit gave a gift to the church in one era, the task to be done was accomplished and perhaps because of the success and dedication of those called to it, the world has moved on. The dynamism of many lay groups and movements in the post-conciliar church owes a debt to a well-educated, effectively catechised laity whose spiritual health has developed at the hands of the religious who have ministered to them. If there is a clear diminishment in the numbers of those called to run Catholic schools, hospitals and social insti-tutions, there is nevertheless evidence to suggest the glimmerings of a rise in vocations to the religious life. But in itself this poses challenges. What are such people being called to, and will they find it in post-conciliar religious life as it is currently constituted? Recent American statistics offer some challenges to those convinced that the renewal over the past fifty years has taken religious unquestionably in the right direction.[1]

It may be that there is not so much a crisis of vocations but a crisis of culture at the heart of religious life in the West. Numerous books have been written which offer shrewd insights from a social science perspective on this question. In the aftermath of the Second Vatican Council religious were overwhelmed by the convergence of tidal waves of social and religious change. The gradual weakening of 'tribal' Catholicism and culturally

---

1. See Mary E. Bendyna and Mary L. Gautier, *Recent Vocations to Religious Life: a Report for the National Religious Vocation Conference, 2009* and http://nrvc.net/english_version/?return_url=english_version

motivated religious commitment coincided with the replacement of many traditional apostolic religious ministries by secular provision. Alongside this the growth of new confidence in the lay vocation, rooted in baptism, and the universal call to holiness advocated in *Lumen Gentium* chapter 5 seemed to take away the space for religious virtuosity previously occupied by religious.[2] Numerous new ecclesial movements also offered an alternative form of consecration, many of them expressing an ecclesiology and a core ideology at odds with the direction in which religious life seemed to be heading. The 'restorationist' flavour of a number of recently-founded religious orders poses a challenge to the whole project of renewal since *Perfectae Caritatis*, and cannot simply be written off wholesale as a neurotic bid for old securities or a neo-conservative digression. Young women and men appear to have largely voted with their feet away from classical religious life, however renewed it might seem to those within it. To discerners now in their twenties the Second Vatican Council and its heroic struggles are part of history, as remote as the battles of World War I are to me, though I dimly remember the council as a small child. If religious are to stand by what they have made of their way of life in the past fifty years, they must offer a coherent response, beyond simple rejection, to the passion and energy of the young Catholics who are joining such 'restorationist' orders.[3]

Within apostolic women's congregations the convergence of global, historic and social factors seems to have hit hardest. While there has been a steadily growing interest in the spiritual heritage of such congregations, expressed in various forms of associate membership, this has not been coupled with a desire to join their way of life as vowed members. The increasing financial, social and sexual autonomy of women since World War II has meant that religious life no longer offers the attractive and viable alternative to marriage and domestic life that it once did. No doubt further studies will emerge that explore the demise of

---

2. See Patricia Wittberg, *From Piety to Professionalism--and Back?: Trans-formations of Organized Religious Virtuosity*, (Lanham, Lexington Books, 2006).
3. Examples of such orders would be the Franciscans of the Renewal, the Community of St John, the Dominican Sisters of Mary, Mother of the Eucharist and others.

apostolic religious life within the context of the women's movement. But the dual backdrop to the Religious Life Colloquium from which this book emerged was the Apostolic Visitation of women religious in the United States and the Ryan Report in Ireland and other revelations of the sexual abuse crisis among religious. Both provoked a torrent of reaction among religious themselves and the wider church and society.

Critics of contemporary women's religious life display a certain hostility to the women's movement and what they detect as its baleful influence upon religious life. This seems to be coinciding with an increasing clericalism and hardening of the arteries within postmodern Catholicism, beset as it is by these current crises. The insights of social anthropology may be helpful here in interpreting the institutional church's closing in on itself. They can be found in the latest books and presentations of a veteran of religious life renewal, Gerard M. Arbuckle.[4]

While post-conciliar popes and those inspired by them repeatedly call for a return to a lost identity among religious, the crisis of confidence in this identity among religious themselves has been evident in the national websites of the Conference of Religious of England and Wales (CoR) or of Ireland (CoRI) up until recently. Anyone searching for information about becoming a religious might be justified in trying these websites as a first port of call. Both advertised a number of worthy social and moral causes upheld by religious: questions of socio-economic justice, ecology, women's issues, social outreach and the like received admirable coverage. But there was an extraordinary reticence regarding the way in which religious life was presented as valid in and of itself. In fact there was little helpful information about how to go about recognising such a vocation and getting support in any discernment process. Religious appeared to be willing to advertise what they did, and the causes they supported, but not what they were. It is tempting to see the causes as displacement activities, supplying some sort of credentials which the vowed life itself did not. Both websites have now been updated, and show a more robust confidence in religious life, but the silence about religious life as such spoke for itself.

---

4. See Gerald A. Arbuckle, *Culture, Inculturation and Theologians: A Postmodern Critique,* (Collegeville, Liturgical Press, 2010).

A similar void seems to lie at the heart of numerous renewal programmes and studies. Some excellent books and courses have emerged that tackle personal development, therapeutic approaches to community life and the vows, various forms of postmodern spirituality, but not all are notable for their theological rigour. While many religious owe a huge debt of gratitude to the works of Sandra Schneiders, Judith Merkle, Joan Chittister, Donna Markham, Gerry Arbuckle and others, a decade has already gone by since much work of substance has been written. While helpful and inspirational, some of this work inevitably reflects a context and reality not that of the other side of the Atlantic.

The Religious Life Institute began with informal discussions among the membership of CoR in 2006. What emerged was a sense that the renewal of religious life in Britain and Ireland needed collaborative work towards a renewed theology of the consecrated life. These discussions echoed similar debates within the Formation Think Tank, mandated by CoR to explore questions of initial and continuous formation among religious. In 2007 the Religious Life Institute was set up in collaboration with Heythrop College, University of London. The RLI's mission was to foster a theological vision of Christian religious life through study and research. It had a further aim of fostering a new generation of writers and experts to help religious look beyond the post-conciliar agenda by generating good materials that reflected this understanding and developing a renewed appreciation of the place of the consecrated life within the church.

By 2010, after a number of highly successful national study days and the inauguration of a course on the theology of religious life at Heythrop, it became clear that the next step was to hold a colloquium, inviting writers to reflect with other participants on current discussions about religious life, towards a new publication. Are we looking at the imminent death of religious life, or at a future full of hope, or at something in between? The RLI study days have revealed a remarkable strength of faith, hope and charity among religious of all ages. They remain a powerful source of inspiration and positive energy within church and society. Hard questions remain, however, to which there are no easy answers. Nevertheless, because they are hard or have no clear answer is not a reason not to ask them.

This book is the beginning of a conversation. It does not provide answers and does not reflect a 'party line' of the RLI or anyone else. There is strong divergence of opinions within it. But if we do not ask the questions we have no hope of finding an answer. We need to take another look, some fifty years after the Council, at the question of renewal. Many who were at its forefront are now gone. Today's context is different, and today's battles are not the same as yesterday's. Just as religious were asked to undertake the sometimes agonising task of change in the 1960s and 70s, perhaps painful changes and re-evaluations are being asked of us now. Did the council bring about a renewal or an implosion of religious life? Who is looking at religious vocation today? What are they seeking, and what are they finding? The lack of a central theology of vocation is certainly one question that needs urgent addressing. Some of the underlying theological questions about religious life within *Lumen Gentium* and *Perfectae Caritatis* never came to a satisfactory conclusion. Perhaps the time has now come to seek further clarification.

Contents

This book is divided into three sections. In Part I, *Fundamental Questions*, Gregory Collins begins by addressing the vacuum in current theologies of religious life. Mary Finbarr Coffey takes issue with the call in *Perfectae Caritatis* for religious to renew their life by a return to their roots, and, by asking how this has turned out in one given context, questions the approach in general. Martin Poulsom and Kate Stogdon enter into dialogue with two contentious issues that have provoked much discussion within religious congregations: creation theology and feminism.

In Part II, *The Once and Future Vocation*, Christopher Jamison, now director of the National Office for Vocation, opens a debate on religious vocations discernment. A lay voice, that of Joanna Gilbert, offers a critique of the current climate within vocations ministry from a particular perspective, while Gerard Dunne gives an example of a way forward from the experience of the Irish Dominican friars.

The final section, *Forward into the Future*, offers something of a response and a challenge to the questions raised in Part II from Gemma Simmonds and a look into the future from a sociological perspective from James Sweeney. We have offered some discussion questions at the end of each chapter in the hope that they may prove a useful basis for group discussions. We welcome responses from groups or individuals as we seek together, in faith and hope, the 'future full of hope' God offered through the prophet Jeremiah in a similar time of crisis.

PART ONE

Religious Life – Fundamental Questions

1

Giving Religious Life a Theology Transfusion

Gregory Collins OSB

Religious life before the reforms of Vatican II offered a neat programme for spiritual perfection, backed up by the clear certainties of a well defined system. Comprising elements such as a counter-cultural garb, sequestered lifestyle, specialist knowledge mediated through a dead language, methodical mapping of the spiritual life and worship controlled by rubric and law, the system was as clear as a manual of neo-scholastic theology and as tightly organised as a Tridentine Mass. In addition, according to St Thomas Aquinas and a host of lesser imitators, religious could be sure that they were doubly consecrated, having received a 'second baptism' through their profession.[1] When the going got tough there was at least the consolation that all one's efforts would be rewarded in the beyond with a double dose of beatitude.

As Sandra Schneiders put it (drawing on St John of the Cross), after the council religious enthusiastically undertook an active night of purgation, taking apart the system that had sheltered them and jettisoning many of the life's outward forms.[2] Yet in addition to the exhilaration of new beginnings, there was also pain in the process. The active night was only the start for the much more bitter night of passive purification that is never far behind. Many watched in dismay as great numbers abandoned not only quasi-monastic forms of religious life but even the very life itself. If, as the council asserted, all Christians are consecrated and called to perfection in baptism – a perfection just as attainable by the married as by religious – why bother maintaining anachronistic spiritual ghettos?

Today's world, however, looks rather different from the way

---

1. Cf A. Kavanagh, 'Notes on the Baptismal Ethos of Monasticism', in S. Parenti *et al*, (eds), *Evlogema: Studies in Honour of Robert Taft SJ*, (Rome, Studia Anselmiana, 1993), pp 235-245.
2. S. Schneiders, *Finding the Treasure*, (New York, Paulist Press, 2000), pp 153-209.

it did just after the council. Globalisation has both broken down frontiers and assisted in the disappearance of local particularities. The worldwide web has speeded up our means of communication, though not without an increase in superficiality. World poverty remains at an appalling level. Sleeping Islam has awakened and become the most significant 'other' with whom we desperately need to dialogue.

In American perception, Islamic fundamentalism has replaced communism as public enemy number one. Economic and political power is shifting to Asia. Post-Christian Europe appears to grow ever more secular while the United States and Africa seem to get ever more religious. Like it or not, we are breathing the air of post-modernity. The secure values of 'modern' culture – progress, enlightenment and rationality – have been replaced by deconstruction, suspicion and fragmentation. Today's world is a complex, shifting reality.

What of the church? The many gains after Vatican II (including liturgical renewal, emphasis on the role of the laity and ecumenical initiatives) abide. Yet while John XXIII preached *aggiornamento* we got John Paul II, the new *Code of Canon Law*, and a universal catechism. Whether one thinks of that as a 'hermeneutic of continuity' or a loss of enthusiasm for renewal depends on one's perspective.

Pope Benedict XVI's powerfully articulated understanding of what the council really meant means that in today's Catholic church one can, without recourse to a time machine, step back to 1962 – complete with maniples, lace, birettas and in some quarters even wimples. Some on the new right seem to want to go back beyond modernity and reinvent the very systems which have been deconstructed. Meanwhile the global crisis over child abuse currently convulsing the Roman Catholic Church has stimulated tentative criticism of the centralised authoritarian ecclesiology canonised at Vatican I. What meaning can religious life carry in the church in such a world of change? Are its traditional symbols, even when purged and re-shaped, able to speak effectively to our time?

We should not underestimate the extent of the recent deconstruction nor fool ourselves into imagining that some simplistic restoration is possible. There can be no going back. The attempted re-invention of 'tradition' generally generates kitsch and kitsch in the spiritual life is particularly debilitating. Deconstruction and purification were right and fitting and they cannot be reversed.

But we also need to be both honest and realistic: some of the deconstruction was at times more like demolition. In addition, some barely surviving forms of religious life are clearly hovering on the verge of extinction, beyond even palliative care. We do ourselves no favours by choosing to dwell in a land of denial. All things created die, including institutes which are no longer required when the needs they were founded to meet are being met in other ways.

But these reflections are directed to those who, having come through the time of deconstruction relatively intact, are still standing and even looking with some degree of hope (and hope-fully) humility toward the future. It is surely time to go forward. We need to get beyond our desolation. We need to recover the meaning of religious life and re-imagine it as a call to holiness, to intimacy with God in the service of Christ's church. We need to rediscover what St Benedict asserts: one can run with expanded heart in the sweetness of love along this way of the Lord's commandments.[3] There is a life beyond the dark night.

A transformed vision is best articulated through a purified language of symbols. What might the traditional symbols of religious life say in a new era and a new context, having been put through the burning fiery furnace of purification? How might they mediate new life and light so as to reshape our vision of religious life today for the glory of God and the future service of Christ's people? Religious life – its symbols, institutions and traditions – is suffering from spiritual anaemia and is in serious need of a theology transfusion. It is striking how little impact the ideas and images which brought so much life and renewal to the church in the twentieth century, certainly one of the greatest eras of theological creativity in the church's history, have had on religious life as such. We need to reflect on this form of life in the light of ideas such as *kenosis* and *koinonia*, in the light of a

---

3. See *The Rule of St Benedict*, (Stanbrook Abbey, 1937), p 5.

renewed theology of salvation, of the liturgy, of ecumenism, inter-religious dialogue and above all of Trinitarian theology. A renewed theology of religious life is needed not to rebuild our holy ghettos but to equip contemporary religious for living and working where they ought to be – on the frontiers of the church's mission to the world.

One popular writer on religious life has wrestled with its place in the church, though in ways which I find confused and confusing.[4] Notwithstanding the often strained relationship it has had with the institutional church throughout the ages, religious life (even in its eremitical and monastic forms) has always been radically ecclesial, dedicated to the service of God within the church. That service may often be a prophetic thorn in the institutional church's side but it will hardly become more effective by pulling the thorn out altogether. We should not forget the fundamental impulse at the centre of religious life: the Spirit-driven search, guided by the gospel, for transforming union with the God and Father of our Lord Jesus Christ in the communion of Christ's people. Yet we ought to make sure that it really is the God of Christian revelation we are serving and not some bland, ersatz new-age divinity projected out of our own needs, whose image might grace a syncretistic Californian ashram. The God of the gospel is no sentimentalised abstraction: this God is about flesh-taking, death and resurrection.

In this discussion I shall suggest five areas where transforming shots of contemporary theology might profitably be injected into the ailing body of religious life. They are: the paschal, pentecostal, Eucharistic, Marian and mystical dimensions of the life. In each case I shall first summarise what these dimensions entail for the church in general and then apply them specifically to religious life as such. It is hard to establish a hierarchy among them since they are so interconnected, having both objective aspects (what God accomplished by redeeming acts) and

---

4. D. Ó Murchú, *Reframing Religious Life*, (London, St Paul's, 1998). While empathising to some extent with Ó Murchú's legitimate frustrations with the church as institution, it is hard to avoid the impression of subjectivism on his part: at times the objective nature of Christianity as a revealed religion seems open to debate; yet at other times Vatican documents are simply invoked to back up a point being made.

subjective repercussions (how this divine activity is received in faith, hope and love and realised in prayer). They are diverse dimensions of a single whole, the one mystery of Christ.

The paschal dimension

The most significant development in twentieth-century Catholic theology was surely the recovery of the paschal mystery as the centre of the Christian faith.[5] The passing over from death to life of the incarnate Son of God was the culmination of the saving acts through which God disclosed himself in sacred history, recreated the world, and redeemed us from sin and death. It is what we celebrate in worship, proclaim in preaching, live in our morality and experience in mystical prayer. As Karl Barth saw so clearly: God's victory over sin and death through Christ's cross and resurrection was a resounding divine 'No!' to our human 'No' and a faithful 'Yes' to God's own covenanted love.[6] From it everything flows. It is the only atmosphere in which authentic Christian faith and life can flourish. God accomplished the paschal mystery through Christ's self-emptying descent from the glory of the Godhead so as to transfigure the human condition from within. The cross and empty tomb are the divine standards given us to assess the authenticity of everything, especially the 'spiritual' and 'religious'. The church as the community of believers called together by the Spirit is baptised into the paschal mystery for, as the hymns of the Byzantine Easter Vigil put it: 'From death to life and from earth to heaven, Christ has brought us rejoicing!'

Since the paschal mystery is the source of all life, religious life has been from its origins indissolubly connected with Christ's death and resurrection. The notion of a bloodless witness borne in 'white martyrdom' developed after the cessation of persecution. Later in monastic tradition forms of religious profession modelled on the rituals of baptism developed. Following

---

5. L. Bouyer's, *The Paschal Mystery*, (London, George Allen & Unwin, 1951), did much to alert the English-speaking Catholic public to this fact but there was scarcely any significant Catholic theologian of the second half of the twentieth century who did not reflect deeply on the paschal mystery. It became a guiding idea at Vatican II.
6. K. Barth, *Dogmatics in Outline*, (London, SCM, 1966), pp 101-108.

the council's assertion of the universal call to holiness and out of respect for the uniqueness of the church's one baptism and the consecration it confers on all Christians, we should not describe religious profession as a 'second baptism'. But neither should we lose the paschal significance of religious life for those who are called to it, for by professing the evangelical counsels religious choose to shape their lives according to the paschal mystery in the paradigmatic self-sacrificial, kenotic pattern of life demonstrated by Christ in his entry into the world, his passion, burial, and descent into hell. The three vows (traditional since the second millennium) might best be seen as a path for practising *kenosis* and being configured by the Holy Spirit to the paschal mystery.

- Freely promised poverty images the progressive stripping of glory undergone by Christ, from his voluntary renunciation of his divine privileges in the incarnation to his enforced denudation on Calvary. Creatively internalised, poverty can remake religious in Christ's image, likening them to the non-grasping Trinitarian God who lets things be, whose inner life consists in sharing, both in time and in eternity.

- Freely chosen chastity can image the pure intensity of Christ's love for the Father, the fact that one enters his community neither by ethnic inclusion nor by the will of the flesh but by a new birth through grace, and invoke the goal awaiting all Christians since the children of heaven are neither given nor taken in marriage. Creatively internalised chastity is essentially a call to mystical union.

- Obedience images the core reality of Christ's paschal mystery: the mission of the Son sent by the Father to redeem us by healing our stubborn self-will and hard-heartedness by his perfect obedience. Creatively internalised obedience recalls the one who came not to do his own will but the will of the one who sent him, and who for that reason was raised from death and exalted into glory.

The pentecostal dimension
Pascha was for Pentecost because the purpose of Christ's saving passage through death was the outpouring of the Holy Spirit,

the breath of divine life, to invigorate the church and reanimate the world. Pentecost universalises the paschal mystery for the Spirit, releases the saving acts of Christ from the constraints of time and space and makes his glorified presence available to the church in liturgy and life as she passes through time and moves towards the *eschaton*. Only in the twentieth century, mostly under Orthodox influence and partly due to charismatic renewal, has pneumatology found its place in Catholic life. Yet the third divine person cannot be controlled or manipulated by any institution or earthly ingenuity: the church must continually ask for his/her presence and gifts afresh in every liturgical celebration. The community of Christ lives by a continuous invocation (*epiklesis*): the Christian life is pentecostal to the praying fingertips of its upturned hands.

Religious life pertains essentially not to the institutional structures of the church but to its pentecostal, charismatic endowments. The original monastic impulse gave rise to lay movements; only later did it become interwoven (for men) with the priesthood and episcopate, leading thereby to many problems of self-definition and identity, and not only for religious. Yet a quick glance at the litany of the saints will verify that throughout history the emergence of new forms of religious life indicates the unquenchable power of the Spirit in raising up 'men and women outstanding in holiness', 'living witnesses' to God's saving power, as the Roman liturgy puts it. In the Christian East religious are seen as those who aim to live directly under the guidance of the Holy Spirit. Orthodox spirituality speaks of becoming a Spirit-bearer, or in the Greek world, a *kaloyer*, a spiritually beautiful elder.[7]

- Such are those religious who, having been tried and tested in conflicts with their own inner demons, dedicated themselves to communion with God and learnt compassion through suffering, become people of perpetual prayer and penetrating wisdom, capable of speaking prophetically within the church.
- Byzantine tradition ascribes to such religious the gift of

---

7. S. Spidlik, *The Spirituality of the Christian East*, (Kalamazoo, 1986), pp 284-285.

> *kardiognosis*, a spiritual clairvoyance enabling them to pierce though appearances and look with mercy into the hearts of others.
> - Freed by grace from all-consuming egoism and with inner senses attuned to the presence of the divine, their lives become a constant communion with God. Invoking the grace of the Holy Spirit within the heart and calling on the name of Jesus they become filters through which divine love is mediated to the people of God.

Today more than ever, in our hyper-institutionalised and over-clericalised Latin church, we need to develop this Eastern understanding of religious life as dedicated charismatic holiness. Yet the Holy Spirit also challenges us as well. Without the fire of the Paraclete, religious life can dissolve into a loveless round of duties and observances or simply dissolve entirely. Dissipating their energies in a rush of activities more or less meritorious, religious can also experience 'burn out' in busy-bodied activism, as bad as one might find in an upwardly-mobile career in the city. Only by constant interaction with the spontaneous promptings of the Spirit without whom nothing is good or holy, can a religious vocation be filled with the breath of divine life.

The Eucharistic dimension
If the source of new life in Christ is the ever-renewed action of the Spirit manifesting the paschal mystery among us, then the Eucharistic assembly is the privileged place where that occurs. Called together by the Spirit and instructed by the proclamation of the word, united in voice and gesture and taken up into Christ's redeeming sacrifice, the Christian community comes into being at every Eucharist. Making the effective memorial (*anamnesis*) of his passion, death and resurrection believers learn to live a eucharistic life. Schooled in thanksgiving, sacrifice, praise and intercession, they are gradually sensitised to the invisible divine presence which impinges on them everywhere, not only during worship but in the liturgy of life itself.

Unfortunately within religious life today, as in the wider church, the sacrament of unity is able to provoke very mixed reactions. After the council, most religious embraced liturgical renewal with enthusiasm, rejoicing in the arrival of the vernacular, appreciative of the new lectionary and enthused by more spontaneous styles of celebration. Yet whether one has 'liberal' or 'neo-conservative' sympathies there is certainly no more problematic area in today's church than the liturgy. The recent restoration of the (unreformed) pre-Vatican II liturgical books, the current disquiet regarding the new English translation of the Roman Missal, but also the persistence of tired and often tedious liturgical bad habits picked up in the nineteen seventies, are only some indications of how deep the division is. For many religious, especially women, the initial enthusiasm perished on various rocks such as gender-exclusive language, clericalism and the issue of women's ministry (or rather the lack thereof).

Those issues will not go away and will eventually have to be faced more imaginatively by the church's authorities. Yet despite difficulties the celebration of the Eucharist remains central to Catholic identity and to being a religious in the church. It embodies the primary Catholic symbol-system. The church both makes the Eucharist and is in turn made by it: we who are many become one body through sharing in the one bread and drinking from the one cup. There can be no substitute for a eucharistic vision, binding together all in Christ, the source of unity. Orthodox Christians speak of the Eucharist as divine medicine, an antidote to the various pathologies afflicting fallen human beings, such life-threatening conditions as fragmentation, isolation and loneliness. All are healed by the inclusive medicine of the Eucharist, the sacrament of communion.

Since the church comes into being at the Eucharist, religious communities which constitute significant cells in the Christian community will also find their origin and meaning at the table of the Lord.

- Regular participation in the Eucharist by religious is a reminder that everything is gift and that grace and gratitude are always interwoven in God's plan. The gift of God's word in holy scripture enlightens them about the divine will for their life and work and its proclamation reactivates the covenant faith of God's people, powerfully symbolised by religious profession.
- The breaking of bread and the sharing of the sacrificial cup which make Christ's self-offering vividly present

remind religious of God's call to offer themselves for service to Christ's people; but also teaches them how to view their vulnerability in the light of his life-giving wounds.

- Religious are commissioned and sent at the conclusion of the Eucharist as witnesses of the resurrection and bearers of the gifts they have received.

Living from the Eucharist as the source of one's religious life should not lead to isolation in ecclesiastical ghettos but to establishing laboratories of common life. Called, enlightened, offered in sacrifice and nourished by their participation at the table of the Lord, religious are united with Christ and sent on mission by the Spirit, in union with one another, their whole congregation and the church – of which their small communities are a living manifestation.

The Marian dimension

Catholic and Orthodox Christianity sees Mary the *Theotokos*, the Mother of the Lord, as the living icon of Christian discipleship. Hans Urs von Balthasar and Adrienne von Speyr have reminded us that the whole church has a Marian dimension which consists in the Christian community itself becoming, through the Spirit's grace, a Godbearer.[8]

Focused on the Lord in liturgical worship, the supreme expression of contemplative receptivity to the Holy Spirit, the church, by witnessing to Christ in daily life through its preaching, service and struggle for God's kingdom, assists the flesh-taking of the Word. But the personal life of Christians also has a profoundly Marian dimension. As spiritual writers, ranging from St Maximus the Confessor, through the medieval mystics asserted every Christian is called to be a virgin consecrated totally to God and a mother giving birth to his Word.

The Marian dimension meant too often in the past that emotionally emasculated men desperate to maintain a jealously-guarded patriarchal *status quo* projected an idealised and imaginary model of the feminine onto women. After forty years of deconstruction we still need to redeem this dimension and restore to it a better understanding.

Creative exegesis of the Lucan annunciation account along

8. A. Von Speyr, *Handmaid of the Lord*, San Francisco, 1985.

with the symbolic presentation of Mary in the fourth gospel highlights paradigmatic features of the discipleship she exemplifies, which are rich in meaning for religious life.

- Mary's courage in welcoming her unique vocation to bring forth Christ makes her an icon of the non-patriarchal fatherhood and motherhood of God ('he' being a 'Father' who gives eternal 'birth' to 'his' 'Son').
- Mary as the greatest of prophets teaches us the covenant faith in the God of Abraham and Sarah, Isaac, Moses and Miriam.
- Mary as icon of the Holy Spirit witnesses through her kenotic self-emptying to the Spirit who in turn points kenotically to Christ …

The mystical dimension

'The mystery' in the New Testament is God's revelation of his hidden plan to unite all things through Christ's death and resurrection. Mystical experience is the secret, inner knowledge of the heart developed through reflection on the testimony to Christ in scripture, liturgical celebration and contemplative prayer. Christ as the incarnate Word is therefore the incarnation of the mystical. Liturgical worship is the church's privileged point of contact with the mystery of salvation. Authentic mysticism drawing life from 'the wellsprings of worship' awakens receptivity to God's presence everywhere since God's glory fills all heaven and earth (Isa 6:1-8).

Living together in communities of mutual support, with a daily rhythm of common worship and regular meditative practice, religious have unique opportunities to contemplate the mystery of Christ in holy scripture as they meet it in the celebration of the liturgy and in engagement with the world. But we need to rejuvenate this mystical dimension.

- The false dichotomy which imagines that singing the divine office, mental prayer or adoration of the Blessed Sacrament are more 'mystical' activities than tending the sick, teaching the young or visiting prisoners needs to be finally abandoned. 'Contemplative' and 'mystical' refer to states of the heart that can flourish in any situation, providing the heart is fixed on God. As Karl Rahner once noted, at the heart of every religious vocation there ought to be a mystical and indeed 'monastic' impulse (in the original sense of 'single-minded').

- Religious are also pioneers who often inhabit liminal zones, frontier-dwellers whose proper place is not so much at the heart of the church (actually occupied by the family, the domestic church) but at its periphery, on the interface between church and world. Religious should therefore be in contact with contemporary expressions of spirituality and the mystical beyond the church – both in secular society and among believers of other faiths.

- They should be people whose task on earth is to bring everything into contact with the Trinity, the one true God who voluntarily leaves the inner sanctum to enter into union with us. That means fostering a mystical type of faith with a non-judgemental, non-proselytising witness to Christ's truth. To do that credibly religious need to be people of profound prayer, meditation, and mystical yearning, ardent lovers of God in whom the authentic mysticism of the gospel, the liturgy and the church can find a ready dwelling place.

The Trinitarian dimension

It is appropriate to conclude these reflections with the Trinitarian dimension. Inevitably, accentuating the paschal and pentecostal dimensions of Christianity led to the most remarkable achievement of modern theology: bringing the doctrine of the Holy Trinity out of the abstraction and oblivion in which it had languished since at least the eighteenth century. All the great theologians of the twentieth century, regardless of denominational allegiance, reflected deeply on the Trinity.

Contemporary theologians emphasise that God self-reveals as a communion (*koinonia*) of divine Persons united in an eternally self-constituting/self-sacrificing web of mutual relationships. God is a flowing circle of inter-penetrating, self-giving lovers, whose source is the first person, the Father. The divine life is a communion of giving and receiving in which Father, Son and Holy Spirit constitute and affirm one another in a union so absolute that with each one dwelling within the others through *perichoresis* (i.e. mutual interpenetration), there is but one subject, God.

This mystery, impenetrable to unaided human reason, God reveals to us through Christ in the Holy Spirit by means of two voluntarily undertaken movements (*kenoses*) disclosing the excess of divine self-emptying love: the incarnation, crucifixion and resurrection of the Word, and the descent of the Holy Spirit. God teaches us what relationship really means. The Trinity invites us in love to enter its communion. Christian living is our graced response to that call for the church as community is (ideally) the place of communion-making, the icon, epiphany and disclosure -zone of divine love made real through acting human subjects.

An authentically Trinitarian vision casts much light on religious life. Many consequences could be identified but three practical ones specifically relating to obedience might especially be associated with each divine person in turn:

- Since there is but one divine will common to all three persons, there is no question of the Father imposing his will on the Son and Holy Spirit. Each person acts in harmony and mutual agreement with the others. The Father revealed in the gospel is far from being a patriarchal tyrant. All who undertake the service of leadership in religious communities ought to aim at conforming to this ideal. Yet we are not of course divine persons. Human communities are always inherently imperfect: as unfinished icons of the Trinity we are always being written. Communion grounded in *kenosis* is natural for God but not for us, at least not since our expulsion from Eden. We have to work hard at *kenosis* if communion is to work. But no one ought to do that as diligently as the person who holds the highly ambiguous name of 'superior'. Inspired by the vision of the Trinity, acting in the likeness of the heavenly Father, 'superiors' will aim to promote the common good and further the community's mission not by coercion or intimidation but through dialogue and consultation.

- Although Christ alone accomplished our salvation in the flesh, it was a work common to all three divine persons.

Religious consciously imbued with a sense of the Trinity will work together in self-emptying ways in carrying out their various missions. There will inevitably be conflict and disagreement, but if the self-emptying paradigm of Christ's *kenosis* is kept before a community's eyes, then communion (*koinonia*) will inevitably follow. Abandonment of wilfulness and synergy of wills following the freely chosen self-limitation displayed by Christ and prescribed by Paul as the charter for Christian community is the only authentic model for religious obedience (Phil 2:1-5). But like that of the Lord Jesus it has to be conscious, voluntary and free.

- St Paul ascribed *koinonia* specifically to the Holy Spirit (2 Cor 13:13); St Augustine described the third divine person as the 'kiss' emerging from the love of the Father and the Son; and the Russian Orthodox theologian Sergius Bulgakov called the Spirit the self-emptying 'kenotic' transparent 'space' across and in which the Father and Son embrace in the joy of exultant love.[9] Community obedience in a Trinitarian mode will seek to inhabit that same 'space' – listening attentively for the voice of the Spirit resounding in the gospel and whispering in the common life and opportunities for mission that daily present themselves. The decisive criterion of authentic obedience in religious communities fired by a vision of the Trinity is this: that all actions and decisions, proceeding from voluntary limitation of self-will (*kenosis*) may generate community (*koinonia*) in the likeness of the self-emptying God revealed in Jesus Christ and the Holy Spirit. It was for this freedom that Christ set us free: 'Where the Spirit of the Lord is, there is freedom' (2 Cor 3:17).

It is my hope that a creative transfusion of theology may help awaken religious to the beauty, dignity and glory of their vocation, a life distinctively dedicated to service of the Trinity who reveals the mystery of divine love in creation and redemption. Religious life in its paschal, pentecostal, eucharistic, Marian and

---

9. S. Bulgakov, *Sophia, The Wisdom of God*, (Hudson, Lindisfarne Press, 1993), pp 48-49.

mystical dimensions finally witnesses to the deepest dimension of all – the kenotic love of the one true God who calls us to kenotic life in community and sends us out in the power of the Spirit as heralds and agents of communion in the world. We religious need to hear that call afresh:

> Sleeper, awake!
> Rise from the dead,
> and Christ will shine on you (Eph 5:14).

Reflection questions

1. 'We need to recover the meaning of religious life and re-imagine it as a call to holiness, to intimacy with God in the service of Christ's church.' What strategies can you imagine that would enable people to recover the meaning of religious life?

2. What are 'the traditional symbols of religious life'? How might they be reinterpreted and re-presented in order to reshape a vision of religious life?

3. 'Religious life has always been radically ecclesial'. What does this mean, and how is it expressed in the way your congregation lives, works and prays?

4. How are the paschal, pentecostal, eucharistic, Marian, mystical and Trinitarian dimensions of religious life apparent within your own charism? How do you experience them today?

2

The Complexities and Difficulties of a Return ad fontes

Mary Finbarr Coffey HC

No statement can adequately express the gift of the Spirit lying behind a religious order; it can be grasped and made perceptible only when we see it expressed in people who try to live it. Within this theological understanding the Second Vatican Council called religious institutes to return to their sources and to re-express the initial inspiration in order to address the drama brought about by the developing split between culture and the gospel.[1] Over fifty years later most religious institutes are still groping for revitalising contact with the spirit of their founders. In part this may be because of the very ambitious nature of this enterprise, involving an attempt to articulate a founding inspiration for the modern cultural identity.[2] Both the terms 'inspiration' and the foundation itself are full of complexities. To this subject I will first turn, before examining the role of memory, the founding identity and the contribution of new members, the competent authority to discern between good inspirations during the founding-time and the influence of context in a return *ad fontes*. For the sake of clarity in expression I have kept to the masculine pronoun throughout this discussion.

1. 'PRIMITIVE INSPIRATION' AND A RELIGIOUS FOUNDING EVENT

In the Beginning: Inspiration and the Rule

In theological theories examining the foundation of a religious institute, it is commonly assumed that this is something stable and assessable. In responding to a foundation, biographical writers like to return to the sources in order to evaluate the

1. *Perfectae Caritatis* in A. Flannery, ed, *Vatican Council II: The Conciliar and Post Conciliar Documents*, (Dublin, Dominican Publications, 1992), pp 611 623.
2. James Hanvey, 'Refounding: Living in the Middle Time,' in *The Way Supplement* 101 (2001), *Refounding: Church and Spirituality*, p 30.

importance beginnings had on the corporate life. When they want to understand a gift of 'primitive inspiration' they tend to concentrate on a founding person receiving an 'inspiration' that acts as a driving motivation towards the foundation. It must not necessarily be that the founding person is 'moved' in this first phase, or set in motion. It may be only in a second moment that the light, becoming more urgent, enables the still vague idea which hitherto had not the power to give itself embodiments. To give one example, this seems to be the case of Paul of the Cross: There was the first phase of inspiration that he received as a young man (born 1694), then he wrote the primitive rule in 1720, that is five years before receiving novices.[3] Although it was a much later version of the rule that was approved (1741) and Paul modified it constantly (destroying the primitive text in the year of his death, 1775), the embodiments in this case came after the Rule was written.

Stanislaus Breton is certain that Paul took counsel; that he questioned himself about the best means to use for the execution of his master idea, that is, 'primordially, his rule, inasmuch as this rule is like the plan of a certain architecture'. Finally, after deliberation and consideration of the external conditions 'which do not depend on Paul's will, he judges the suitability and selects the instrumental ensemble which, all things considered, would seem to him more suited to the end he intended'.[4] Religious writers concentrate on the rule and have repeatedly located a founding inspiration in a period prior to writing of the rule.

In the beginning: inspiration and mission tied to fundamental purpose
While most foundations have begun with a rule, it must be noted that this does not apply to all. In the establishment of a foundation without a rule it is normally the existential mission tied to a fundamental purpose and project that takes precedence. Inspiration is equally at work in this instance, understood here as a particular divine impulse to speak, write or act in certain ways. It is a permanent element conceived from the onset in the

---

3. E. A. Livingstone, ed, *The Oxford Dictionary of the Christian Church*, (Oxford, OUP, 1997), p 1241.
4. Stanislaus Breton, *The Passionist Congregation and Its Charism: Studies in Passionist History and Spirituality*, (Rome: Passionist Generalate 1987), pp 1-7.

development of a religious foundation. A second element in a religious foundation is the objective historical world as the terrain in which a 'primitive inspiration' receives its embodiment in the founding time. A final element in the founding of a religious institute is the unique personalities of those who constitute the ecclesiastical group in a diocese or local church as well as the personalities of the founding group itself.

The primitive inspiration thus enters the world through the founding generation, with the founder emerging as the person with the initial inspiration. This person may struggle to find concrete forms for the inspiration and in the struggle come to understand the mission of the institute and the world around more clearly. The narratives he constructs, promotes or which are eclipsed may be understood not only as giving expression to the primitive inspiration, but also as part of the 'framework' that makes the founding identity clearer to him as well as to others.[5] The founder may be understood as interpreting a particular divine impulse in a way that is analogous to a reader who participates in creating the meaning of a literary text through interpretation. The founding generation – indeed also subsequent generations – 'participate' in inspiration in this way. The manner in which a founder fulfils this task differs from that of a group in another historical period or in another location.

At the same time, it is important to point out that the one who is founding does not interpret the meaning of the gift of 'primitive inspiration' entirely subjectively. The historical context, with its contending influences operative in church and state, together with social needs, not only help to form the founding persons of our investigation, but also provide them with a positive direction for interpreting the original inspiration.[6] A founding generation in a religious institute assumes the existence of a liberating God, whose action working through them enables them to carry out their mission.

5. Daniel Speed Thompson, *The Language of Dissent: Edward Schillebeeckx on the Crisis of Authority in the Catholic Church*, (Notre Dame, University of Notre Dame Press, 2003), p 25.
6. Ibid, p 28.

2. FOUNDING THEORIES

Both models incorporate the idea that certain factors have important bearings on the decisions of the founding person and that his understanding of the total situation will determine how he acts. More 'intellectual' theories assume that the founder's understanding of the primitive inspiration will determine the way in which the foundation is established. He will always follow his understanding of what the inspiration and the external situation mean. An existentialist model argues, however, that when the founder deliberates about a choice of embodiments for the initial inspiration, the objective circumstances confronting him in this choice are not clear-cut. He interprets the meaning of the initial inspiration and can re-think the significance of the founding event throughout the entire epoch of the founding person. He can see that goals he is attracted to are more ambiguous than might have been imagined; he is able to make new priorities among the goals he already set; he can even be faced with new goals he had not considered before which require fresh decisions. Thus a primitive inspiration is not fully determined. God's inspiration remains whole, perfect and intact. It is left to the founder to interpret and channel it, under the guidance of the Spirit. The founding decision taken at the historical origins is nonetheless definitive. From the point of view of historical origins, it was the genuine defining decision taken by the founding person and confirmed by the church that is binding on future history. In order that there be continuity in identity across changes in historical circumstances all that is required is that subsequent decisions lie within the genuine possibilities given by an Institute's defining origins and that they do not contradict the origins, in particular in relation to the mission and purpose. This leads us to consider the reality of contest in a founding event.

3. THE MENZINGEN INSTITUTE:
A CASE STUDY: A CONTESTED FOUNDING EVENT (1844-1863)

Fr John Joseph Röllin and Dean von Haller – priests of the diocese of Basel/Switzerland – together with Fr Theodosius Florentini OFM Cap. gave response to what they believed to be a need of the time and established an Institute of Teaching-Sisters in the village of Menzingen Canton Zug, Switzerland (8 August 1844).

In November Sisters Bernarda Heimgartner, Feliciana Kramer and Cornelia Mäder (the first three members) began a school for girls in the village. On his own volition Fr Theodosius wrote Constitutions (1844-1845) and gave the institute the Rule of the Third Order of Leo X (1521). This institute expanded rapidly, with the invitation to open schools addressed by parish priests in surrounding Swiss villages. The extant discourse of Mother Bernarda (first superior) demonstrates that she and the founding sisters believed that the purpose of the new institute – the education of the female youth – was 'a work of God'. Initially Fr Theodosius appeared to have agreed with this, but from the late 1840s onwards we note growing tension.

The Menzingen founding inspiration was in certain conflict between Mother Bernarda Heimgartner and Father Theodosius Florentini. This involved a problem of divergence of purpose and the imposition of additional purposes by Father Theodosius. Examination of attempts to diversify the purpose during the foundation period discloses that this woman of determination was very sure that the mission of holistic Christian education was the will of God for the Menzingen Institute. Bernarda Heimgartner did not accept additional purposes because she knew intuitively that remaining with one purpose was what she had to do; she knew that the identity of the institute was tied to this. Moreover, this one mission was ratified as normative by the Bishops of Basel and Chur in January 1857. Such confirmation notwithstanding, two small factions developed among members of the institute, splintering unity in a corporate self-understanding towards the end of Bernarda's life. Suppression of the founding identity resulted, and the marginalisation of the memory of the spirited foundress continued throughout the reception-history and contributed to a certain distortion, which remains in the institute's corporate memory.

Conflict between the founding inspiration and the constitutions
The primitive inspiration of the institute, as interpreted by Bernarda Heimgartner and the founding sisters was innovative and emancipatory. It seemed to stand in a certain submerged contest with ambiguity and at least one restoration model in the Menzingen Constitutions. Ambiguity was present to the extent

that its author, Fr Theodosius, did not seem to know whether to follow a Jesuit or a mendicant-monastic strain in the text. Two models of religious life were present in submerged conflict during the founding time both within the constitutions and between the constitutions and the lived experience of the sisters. But Bernarda Heimgartner and the founding generation of sisters worked within a broad, flexible framework thanks to an existing vacuum in canon law. They regarded the constitutions as important, but understood them as designed for adaptation to changing circumstances, regarding them neither as sacred text nor rule. The claim that they lived within the cramped conditions of the constitutions was only part of the story at best. Bernarda Heimgartner was a woman of 'spirit' who, in pursuing the purpose of education of the female youth, found a variety of ways to exercise her gifts of leadership.

Menzingen is one case of these particular features of nineteenth and twentieth-century religious foundations.

A primitive inspiration and contest

A 'primitive inspiration' has to find its place in the world in dialogue, and in contest with conversation partners, some of whom place considerable pressure upon its embodiments. External pressures are necessary before an inspiration can find embodiments in the world. Indeed it is these pressures that can test the strength of an inspiration. In the Menzingen founding event (1844-1863) we witness a developing struggle to receive and give expression to a gift of the Spirit. Bernarda Heimgartner's determination and persistence in the contest led to disturbance during the founding time. Moreover, this case study raises the question of whether a primitive inspiration of this nature is inherently contestable. The study would suggest that it probably is, because it holds at its origin an inspiration that comes from the Spirit and it is received in peoples' historical circumstances. Certain conditions will place pressures upon it; therefore there is an inevitable contestability about an inspiration of this kind; it is not a pure entity. This was the pattern of Jesus' proclamation of the kingdom of God. A saving force unleashed by God in history through the life of Jesus remained inherently contestable right to the moment when his human life ended. The contest continues. Religious orders would do well to keep this in mind as they seek to re-found by returning to their own memory. A re-expression of a founding inspiration for mission will inevitably face considerable pressure from post-modernism. For such adherents the religious founding event grounded in the Bible and the Christ event, has no special status over and against other texts or discourses.

4. THE EFFECTS OF ECCLESIAL UNDERSTANDINGS OF RELIGIOUS LIFE ON THE MENZINGEN MEMORY

Gradual church movement towards standardisation of religious life culminated in 1900 with the promulgation of the papal bull *Conditae a Christo.* Here the church required that those institutes who had just been designated as religious return to their constitutions and rule and not *ad fontes*. In stating this, the church identified the essence of the religious life to be expressed in the constitutions and rule, rather than in the lived experience of the founding generation. This posed an obstacle for the identity and memory of the Menzingen Institute being properly understood. Thus the first published history of the institute claimed the revised constitutions of 1901 formed the basis of the Menzingen Institute because this text continued the founding spirit, which was believed to have been incarnated in the first Menzingen Constitutions.[7] The ecclesial way of framing religious life thus influenced the way in which the memory was articulated and held. From the time of the Menzingen foundation in 1844 until 1900, the way in which women's congregations were thought about was loose and fluid, while the first two-thirds of the twentieth century were marked by rigidity in that regard. The Second Vatican Council opened issues of memory and identity, through the way in which the religious founding event itself came into prominence in *Perfectae Caritatis*. As they sought to adapt to the evolving social context, members were advised to return to the original inspiration of the institute, understood as the work of the Holy Spirit.

> It is for the good of the church that Institutes have their own proper characters and functions. Therefore the spirit and

---

7. Rudolf Henggeler, *Das Institut der Lehrschwestern vom Heiligen Kreuz in Menzingen* (Kt Zug), (Menzingen, 1944), pp 238-242.

aims of each founder should be faithfully accepted and retained, as indeed each Institute's sound traditions, all of these constitute the patrimony of the Institute (*Perfectae Caritatis*, 2b).

Notwithstanding this, the Menzingen Institute did not investigate the religious founding event itself, but continued to identify with the narrative established in the first half of the twentieth century. Draft texts of the Menzingen Reform Chapter of 1977 built on the presupposition that the institute's identity was enshrined in the first Menzingen Constitutions (1852) and in the Third Order Rule of Pope Leo X (1521).

5. THE DISTORTING EFFECTS OF MEMORY

When a rule is adopted after the mission of an institute has been determined, what happens sometimes may be compared to the grafting on of an incompatible branch, where there has not been organic growth. The result of this is apparent in the eclipsing or the distorting of the original purpose or aim. In the case of the Menzingen Institute, after the founding time and some time later in the reception history, the original purpose was overlaid by the grafted-on Franciscan Rule. In this case, a loss of the original founding spirit and a certain distortion in the memory was a result.

To establish from a religious founding event an aspect that was central to identity and to show that the subsequent memory distorted this aspect implies an understanding of the mission and identity of the institute as being tied to a fundamental purpose. The Menzingen founding identity was established around education. A distorted memory was subsequently built apart from this identity. Since education in this institute can be regarded as established and justified by its origins, this is the key to the institute's contemporary mission. A study of education in the institute would seem to be a requirement, one which takes into account both a changing world and an ongoing identity because both belong to history. What is the nature of the educational mission in the current circumstances which are so different from those in which Mother Bernarda found herself? Which are the appropriate ministries to be selected for this one mission, in a context that differs substantially from the nineteenth century? These are some of the urgent questions facing the institute.

6. MENZINGEN AND THE CHALLENGES OF THE VATICAN II MANDATE

The Menzingen Institute can be considered a case study of the challenges in meeting the Vatican II mandate and some of the basic lessons that ensue from this study. First, there are non-resolved problems between the original mission and the reception history of the institute. The concern of whether aspects of their current works are in accord with their mission as given in their founding also troubles other religious congregations, because history demonstrates that they may have been pushed into situations that they had not necessarily chosen, but had been constrained for one reason or another. To establish from a founding event that there was some aspect central to identity and to show that subsequent memory involved a distortion around that aspect does raise questions needing to be clarified.

All religious orders (including Menzingen) face Vatican II's challenge to return *ad fontes* and to renew in relation to contemporary needs. The return *ad fontes* is complicated by the nature of the historical character of memory, which generally involves some measure of distortion of the *ad fontes*, and in the case of Menzingen a significant distortion. Return *ad fontes* and *aggiornamento* or learning how to respond with daring to the insistent challenge of the present and future needs of contemporary society are also in a relationship of some tension. One leads potentially to restorationism and the other to dispersal of identity. The renewal of a religious institute requires a creative balance of both approaches. This was the general approach of Vatican II and it would seem to be sound.

7. THE CHRIST EVENT AND THE FOUNDING IDENTITY OF RELIGIOUS INSTITUTES

Founding identity and the contribution of new members
How far is it true to say that the identity of a religious order changes with each person who enters, who adds something new? Each member of the church has a personal vocation and, called to be a member of the church, therefore brings something new at least in one sense, but the church retains its founding identity. It

cannot be said, however, that the church comes to birth through its members.

In a certain sense the Catholic church is not complete: *Lumen Gentium* tells us that the church of Christ subsists in the Catholic church (*Lumen Gentium*, 8). On the one hand, the church is endowed by Christ with all the means necessary for salvation and it has these means indefectibly. On the other hand, we can say that its fullness of realisation is still to be achieved, of which a most obvious example is the exercise of certain virtues found sometimes outside the Catholic church in even greater abundance. For example, evangelical Christians outside the bounds of full communion often exhibit greater commitment to mission. In the understanding of Vatican II such virtues belong to the church of Christ and therefore impel towards Christian unity. The development of dogma offers another model. Revelation is complete in Jesus Christ with the death of the last apostle until the *parousia*. Yet every Christian thinker can bring something new, by bringing to prominence something that had been lying in the background, thus offering richer insight into the Christ event.

These models may be understood as useful analogues to consider the way in which entrants can bring something new. They are not going to change the essence of a founding identity, but they can contribute to its building up in terms of outreach, membership, but also in ennobling the founding inspiration by bringing elements to the fore that may be underdeveloped.

Caution is required when applying these models outside of divine revelation, even when *Perfectae Caritatis* seems to imply that there is a definitive closure to a founding inspiration (2b). There is an historical event that is the Christ event, which includes the paschal mystery and the canon of scripture. There is a clear understanding that this event is complete with the foundation of church – the Body of Christ – and requires no addition. Nothing more can be added to Christ's revelation. Whether one can add anything to the Rule of St Francis is another question. We cannot claim that the Franciscan founding event was the last word in the same way in which we claim that Jesus Christ is the *alpha* and *omega*. In other words, we cannot argue for an analogy between a divine institution and a divinely prompted human institution.

All committed members make a positive contribution to the development of a founding inspiration, but some are of greater influence and significance. Thomas Aquinas, for instance, made an enormous theological contribution and to ignore his contribution in the Dominican Order by returning only to Dominic would be an error and would therefore miss the point. St Dominic can only act as a lens to bring Christ more into focus, but Thomas Aquinas does more than bring Dominic into focus. This means that founders focus the mystery of Christ for members of a religious order, but members of the order do more than focus on an aspect of a founder and indeed they should note the dangers of confining themselves in a cult of the founder.

There has to be something that is of the essence of a founding inspiration that cannot be lost without losing the original inspiration itself. Should this happen, the original inspiration can no longer be known or recognised and the original calling from God is ignored. In other words, the resultant changes in the institute have not been faithful to the founding inspiration. It is no longer what it started out to be and there has to be the recognition that what happened initially is not properly the founding inspiration or the founding event of an institute that subsequently took on a different nature and character. Does every individual bring something to a religious order? The answer is yes, but every individual may not necessarily contribute something new. This is because, other than the event of Jesus Christ, no other founding event has that absolute nature. But if a founding event is not absolute it is definitive and within that every committed member has something to contribute.

Inspiration? Tradition? Authority? Experience? Who decides?
After the Christ founding event what followed immediately was oral tradition subsequently committed to writing. Whether or not revelation is contained in scripture and in what sense it is continuing is a distinctly open question. Nevertheless, it is the ongoing stream of traditions of the first Christian communities that is ingrained in scripture. In *Dei Verbum* the importance of tradition is explained and it is stated that tradition is the integral handing on of revelation (*Dei Verbum*, 9). Vatican II thus makes a high claim for tradition in some ways, but does not of course equate it with the Word of God. How does this claim for

tradition illumine the question of a founding event of a religious institute and its reception history?

Inspiration likewise establishes a tradition. The Menzingen primitive inspiration gives authority to its early traditions, acknowledging that its founding event came first, showing clearly that a temporal priority was given to this. Moreover, this founding event ran its course from 1844-1863 and yielded very little influence on the constitutions. Instead there was contest between them to a significant extent. On the other hand the letters of the foundress and the chronicle of the institute each reflect the ongoing stream in which the Menzingen primitive inspiration found concrete embodiments. What part of the institute, what unforgettable part dwells in the memory mirrored in these texts? We have to recognise a return *ad fontes* as a process of the founding event and its reception history. The task of reception can be an event repeated over a number of centuries down to our own day, and it is part of making an institute what it is. Reception must not involve distortion. A return *ad fontes* can never mean merely suggesting new equivalent forms. It means a journey back through memory, enabling the founding inspiration to come alive in our own modes of thinking, and appealing to tradition in a bid to ensure that this unique founding memory resounds in the forms of our own era. This is a risky business, but the very risk is the basis of its success.

Arguably, just as the gospels contain a reflection of the life of the early Christian communities, so too, do the letters of the foundress and the chronicle contain a description of the early Menzingen mission and purpose and thus of the early Menzingen founding inspiration. Here I am taking the letters of the foundress and the chronicle as analogous to scriptures, and the Menzingen founding event itself as analogous to the early church traditions within the communities out of which the scriptures developed. Before his death Jesus assured his disciples that the Spirit would teach them all that he had said to them and that they would also do greater things, since the Spirit would tell them the truth that Jesus never told them (Jn 16:13). In the light of the Spirit, a return *ad fontes* involves religious in more than an examination of texts; rather it involves a journey back through memory to their originating inspiration and to greater understanding of this gift of the Spirit for mission in the contemporary world.

A dispute about the purpose of Menzingen Institute was resolved by the bishops of Basel and Chur (1857), thereby showing the wider church acting as the competent authority to discern between good inspirations. The bishops thus judged what was in accord with the primitive inspiration and to be followed by a particular religious institute. Can we say that the actions of the bishops contributed to the foundation of the Menzingen identity or were these actions simply confirmation of an already existing identity? In fact it seems to be both, contribution and confirmation, just as the decision made at the Council of Jerusalem was part of making the church what it is and confirming what it already was.[8] Thus the founding event may be definitively understood as the working of the Holy Spirit. In turn this would also tend towards the view that there may be thought present within the founding event and in the writings that the human founders were not aware of. This suggests that those who enter an order subsequently can draw out something that is not radically new. Significant elements can be exposed and realised, but need to be tested against the founding inspiration itself. It is the task of the general chapter and of the church to decide whether or not what is proposed is the work of the Spirit in a particular Institute.

8. SOCIAL CONTEXT CHALLENGES A RETURN AD FONTES

The formal challenge addressed by the Second Vatican Council to religious can be read no longer in a departing Tridentine church, responding to modernity, but in the context of a post-Vatican II church, caught in a struggle with a new world context.[9] This struggle is partly constituted by the context which tends to be overladen with the quest for personal autonomy and freedom,

8. The essence of the church was not open at the Council of Jerusalem, but arguably whether or not Gentile Christians had to observe the Mosaic Law of the Jews was an open question before the council. We can say therefore, that the decision of the Council of Jerusalem is part of making the church what it is, in a way that the decision of the Council of Nicea was not. In the case of Jerusalem the act of the magisterium can be considered constitutive as well as definitive. The Jerusalem Council was held around AD 50; Acts 15:1-39.
9. Hanvey, 'Refounding', p 30.

especially in the West. There is the gospel, on the one hand, which 'embodies a claim to absolute truth (about God and God's purpose) and the imperative to proclaim it.'[10] On the other hand, there is a context which tends to understand the self as the product of a range of choices, with all previous values and obligations transforming into ever new options.[11] Here forgetting rather than remembering seems to be important.[12] The claim that the past can influence the present and future identity of a religious order constitutes a position which stands inevitably in strong tension with certain social norms in contemporary society.

Reflection questions

1. The return to sources is described here as 'an attempt to articulate a founding inspiration for the modern cultural identity'. How has your congregation tried to do this?

2. The author also points to the historical context of the foundation as providing a positive direction for interpreting the original inspiration. How has this changed with the challenges of today's different contexts?

3. The author points to a certain tension between the council's call both to a return *ad fontes* and to *aggiornamento*, as leading potentially either to restorationism or to dispersal of identity. Have you experienced this tension? How has it manifested itself?

---

10. James Sweeney *et al*, general eds, *Going Forth: an Enquiry into Evangelization and Renewal in the Roman Catholic Church in England & Wales. Research Report*, (Cambridge, Von Hügel Institute and Margaret Beaufort Institute of Theology), November 2006, p 23.

11. Kevin Vanhoozer, ed, *The Cambridge Companion to Postmodern Theology* (Cambridge, Cambridge University Press, 2003), pp 9-25.

12. Tiemo Rainer Peters and Claus Urban, *Ende der Zeit? Die Provokation der Rede von Gott* (Mainz, Matthias-Grünewald-Verlag 1999), pp 34-36.

3

Sustaining Presence:
Religious Life in the Midst of Creation

Martin Poulsom SDB

If there is any biblical model that has shaped the twenty years or so that I have lived as a religious, it is that of Exodus. This narrative has played a key role in the accounts of religious life in the twentieth century that I have heard from religious a generation or two older than me. These stories have, in my own experience, often been filtered through the readings of Exodus presented by theologians of liberation. Their understanding of the God who wants to give life and freedom to all has been a powerful influence on my own living of the vows, inspired by stories of liberation told by those who have gone before me. For many of them, the Exodus narrative describes their experience after Vatican II with great insight, as the heady sense of freedom immediately following the council gave way to forty years of wandering in the wilderness, being slowly guided by God towards a land of promise.

Religious of my own generation, however, have a different experience of this period of time. We never knew the pre-conciliar church, because we were born during or after the council. (I was born in 1965, a month or so before the publication of *Gaudium et Spes*, the last of the major decrees of Vatican II.) The church and the religious life in which I have lived is post-conciliar. I am just about old enough to have been present at Mass before the first edition of the Roman Missal in English in 1970, but have no memory of these liturgies. My mother – and, incidentally, my father, too, at my mother's insistence – was 'churched' when I was born before she could return to the sacraments, but by the time my sister was born eighteen months later, this practice had been abandoned. To use the imagery of Exodus again, religious of my generation are like the children of Israel who were born in the wilderness. Our view of the Promised Land is bound to differ from that of our older brothers and sisters, if only because we have had no first-hand experience either of the relative plenty of Egypt, or of the trials and tribulations that were experienced there.

One of the ways that the relative plenty of pre-conciliar religious life found expression was in the image of religious as a workforce, a group of people who, because of their numbers in the church, were able to do things that otherwise could not have been done. Some congregations – including my own – were at the forefront of establishing Catholic schools in Britain and Ireland as the nineteenth century moved into the twentieth. Others founded Catholic hospitals, where they were able to tend the poor in the years before a National Health Service was established. This image of religious as a workforce would surely also have been buttressed by the post-war influx of members into many congregations, which went hand-in-hand with a rise in the number of young men entering seminaries. Paul Murray notes that a major extension of the seminary at Ushaw, near Durham, was undertaken in the early 1960s. At its peak, it accommodated more than four hundred junior and senior seminarians, compared to the twenty or thirty there before its closure as a seminary.[1] However, as Sandra Schneiders observes, simply comparing the years of plenty immediately before the Council with today's wilderness years is short-sighted, since it ignores what she calls 'the vocational tsumani beginning in the 1940s and peaking in the mid-1960s'. She points out that the number of women religious in the United States of America between the 1700s and the early 1900s 'was nowhere near the post-war high point. Indeed, it was closer to today's "low point".'[2] All the same, the life experience of religious who have lived through the time of the council has led many of them to set aside the image of the workforce, since it describes neither the religious life they are now living nor that to which they feel called by the God of Exodus. In its place, two different images seem to have developed, each of which marks out a distinctive path through the wilderness in fidelity to Vatican II.

The first is that of the religious as a mystic, someone who is

1. Paul Murray, 'The Need for an Integrated Theology of Ministry within Contemporary Catholicism', *Concilium* 2010/1, pp 43-54, 45.
2. Sandra M. Schneiders, 'Why we Stay(ed)', *Concilium* 2010/1, pp 119-30, 125.

focused more on being than doing. As numbers decreased remarkably in the years after Vatican II and the workforce image became unsustainable, these religious became more and more aware of the flaws in the work-centred, mission-driven approach that the image had generated. Inspired by the council, they engaged in the task of *ressourcement*, discovering in new ways not only the founding principles of their congregations, but also the depth and richness of Catholic spirituality as a whole. As they deepened the contemplative aspects of their calling as religious, they came to realise that a sense of worth born principally out of a work-ethic was foreign to who they were called to be. These religious developed a mystical approach to life that was deeply counter-cultural, particularly in the performance -driven, ultra-consumerist 1980s. One of the fruits of their mystical turn was a radical awareness of the presence of God in all things, a presence that sustained them through the social, cultural and ecclesial changes they faced. This sense of God's presence was palpable to others and inspired some, at least, to follow them into religious life, seeking a similar depth of awareness of God in their lives. These religious also became a source of inspiration to the lay men and women around them who had taken up many of their ministries, powerfully reminding them that who we are is not made secure by what we do.

The other image, which developed alongside this one, kept something of an emphasis on action, but transformed it in response to the signs of the times. As a result of this dialogue with a changing situation both in the church and in the world, these religious came to see themselves as prophets, called to be radically open to the voice of God and to speak out without fear. They grew into vocal and persuasive witnesses for Conciliar *aggiorna-mento*, bringing the Word of God and the gifts of their renewed constitutions into a dynamic interrelationship that was a powerful force for renewal. Many of them became charismatic leaders in the midst of great challenge and difficulty. Like their founders and foundresses before them, they took religious life to the margins of church and society, responding generously to the call to be a voice for the voiceless, to engage in ministries that few others were willing to undertake. For at least a few young men and women – myself among them – they were beacons of hope, proclaiming a way to the Promised Land in the midst of so much struggle and loss. Their pioneering work for the homeless, their championing of justice and peace, their challenge to think globally and act locally, have left an enduring legacy of prophetic action that has inspired many to do likewise.

More recently, some members of both groups have responded to the situation of climate change and biodiversity loss facing the planet as a whole, but in two rather different ways. Those inspired by a more mystical and contemplative approach to religious life have deepened their awareness of the presence of God in nature through creation spirituality. These religious have drawn extensively on the historical resources that nourished their mystical development in order to articulate how we can live in greater harmony with the natural world. This process has been rich and diverse, drawing from the whole of Christian history and open to much wisdom from elsewhere. Two medieval figures who have been sources of inspiration to many religious in this regard are Francis of Assisi and Hildegard of Bingen. Francis has a keen sense of God's presence in nature, perhaps most clearly expressed in his *Canticle of Brother Sun*, in which he is inspired even to call death his sister. Hildegard sees such a close connection between the life that God gives to the natural world and that which he offers to the mystic that she coins a new word to describe it. She speaks of God's *viriditas* (greening power), a term that she uses not only to describe creation, but also the growth in virtue and holiness that God gives to the soul.

Those religious whose development has taken a more prophetic form have also responded to these planet-wide challenges, drawing attention to the fact that it is the poor who are hit first and worst by the effects of climate change, even though they have done the least to cause it. Drawing on the rich heritage of prophetic imagery found in scripture, they have challenged us to recognise the hardness of heart that has often characterised our attitude towards the natural world. They have boldly pointed out the uncomfortable truth that if we do not change, the future of the ecosystem in which we live is at risk. Their witness calls us all to conversion, to a change of heart, to widen our sphere of concern, not just from the local to the global human family, but in a way that expresses solidarity with all creation. They invite us to see clearly where we are going and to change the path we are on, walking forward with courage, even if we sometimes feel that there are too few of us to really make much of a difference. They call us to listen for the voice of God as we travel, bidding us to commit ourselves to nurturing life to the full for all God's creatures, especially the weakest and most vulnerable.

The responses of both these groups, initially to the challenges facing religious life after Vatican II and, more recently, to the task of articulating a religious life in the midst of creation, have brought much richness and much that it is of lasting value. However, it is also important to note that, as the two images have developed, as the two paths of fidelity to Vatican II have been trodden, they have diverged significantly. As a result, being and doing are sundered from one another – or, to use their more traditional names, the paths of contemplation and action seem to have become an either/or choice. This is an unhappy separation of themes that are intrinsically interrelated in the constitutions of so many religious orders and congregations, whether of monastic, mendicant or apostolic origin. It is a separation which may well be a sign of our times, since it has taken place along the same fault lines that separate *ressourcement* and *aggiornamento* as opposing ways of interpreting Vatican II. This does not mean, however, that divergence is the only way forward.

The task facing my own generation of religious is, therefore, far more challenging than simply labelling the Exodus model as part of the 'hermeneutic of discontinuity' and discarding it. It seems to me that what we are called to do is to try to find ways of crafting anew the language we use about religious life so that traditional ways of speaking about contemplation and action can hang together intelligibly once again.[4]

One possible starting point for this task, theologically, could be a consideration of how being and doing are related in God, in whose image humanity is created (Gen 1:27). Many Catholic

---

4. cf. Kathryn Tanner's use of similar language to describe the challenge that contemporary theologians face in their attempts to speak about God and creation today in Kathryn Tanner, *God and Creation in Christian Theology: Tyranny or Empowerment?* (Oxford: Blackwell, 1988), p 169.

theologians down through the ages have noted that God is being itself. God's essence is God's existence, as Aquinas put it. He deliberately used the Latin word *esse* to denote God's existence, so as to stress that the perfect being of God is not static, but intrinsically dynamic. *Esse* is a verb, not a noun, so God's very nature is to-be. God's being is inherently active. The implication of Aquinas' use of *esse* is that God can be said to be existence as act: God is being-in-act.[5] Karl Rahner puts this the other way round, in his description of God as a Trinity of persons. When God reveals himself to humanity, God reveals who he is in and through what he does. This mutual interaction between being and doing, in which each finds both its expression and its fulfilment in the other, can be a useful resource for both mystical and prophetic religious. It can prevent prophetic action from degenerating into mere activism and mystical being from degenerating into an inactive 'being there'.

In order to truly live in the image and likeness of God, our being and doing ought to be intrinsically interrelated, too. Mystical and prophetic liberation can and should go hand in hand, since the God of liberation calls us to both. According to Edward Schillebeeckx, the way that this connection makes itself visible in the years around the time of the council is in the interaction between mysticism and politics. As a Dominican, he sees these as contemporary expressions of contemplation and action, features of religious life that are central to his mendicant inheritance and inseparable from one another if that life is to be lived in all its fullness. He notes that this interplay between contemplation and action can be present in the lives of all people of faith. It is not only unnecessary, but, more importantly, unhelpful to completely separate mystics and politicians from one another in our thinking or practice. If we do, we all too easily over-professionalise them. This results in seeing mysticism and politics as the domain of a small number of people who live these lives in an exemplary way, so that the rest of us don't have to.[6]

Instead of this, he recommends that we think of mysticism

5. David B. Burrell, *Knowing the Unknowable God: Ibn-Sina, Maimonides, Aquinas* (Notre Dame: University of Notre Dame Press, 1986), pp 29-30.
6. Edward Schillebeeckx, *Church: the Human Story of God,* (London: SCM Press; New York: Crossroad, 1990), pp 66-72.

and politics as aspects of the life of faith as a whole, rather than being separate components that must somehow be brought together. His markedly non-dualistic approach speaks of mysticism as 'an intensive form of experience of God or love of God'. It is an intensification of elements that are – or ought to be, at any rate – present in the lives of all believers. Similarly, he calls politics 'an intensive form of social commitment' and, as a result, not something that is the exclusive domain of professional politicians. All Christians are called to play their part in making a better future, through prophetic participation in culture and society.[7] Timothy Radcliffe, a fellow Dominican, makes a similar point when he speaks about the interplay between action and prayer in the life of the Christian: 'Our actions are prayers – they beseech God to do something – and our prayers are actions, which may have real effects.'[8]

The interplay between mysticism and politics, contemplation and action, that these authors invite us to participate in, reveals some of the important features of a religious life in the midst of creation. It is not possible at this stage to give a definitive account of what religious life will look like if it takes up this invitation, since a clear picture will only emerge as we engage in the creative task of making it a reality. However, an outline sketch, suggesting possible lines of development, is certainly appropriate at this stage. The first thing to note is that evolving such an interplay is both affirming and challenging to the two groups of religious that I have characterised as mystical and prophetic. On the one hand, it invites religious to a more intense experience of God the Creator and of love for all that God has made. On the other hand, it summons us to develop a more intensive form, not only of social and political commitment, but of ecological commitment, too – a living and vibrant care for creation.

This mutual enrichment calls each group deeper into its particular giftedness, enriching their established emphasis with elements from the charism of the other group. As such, it could also serve as a unifying process for the two groups

7. Edward Schillebeeckx, *Jesus in Our Western Culture: Mysticism, Ethics and Politics,* (London: SCM Press, 1987), pp 71-72.
8. Timothy Radcliffe, *Why Go to Church? The Drama of the Eucharist* (London: Continuum, 2008), p 95.

themselves, drawing them into deeper communion with each other and making their joint witness to the gospel more fruitful. The prophetic group are right to say that their emphasis on social and political liberation is an indispensable part of the gospel, a symbol of the life-giving presence of the kingdom in the world. It is also true that the absolute presence of the creating and saving God lies at the very heart of this process of liberation. A deeper awareness of God's presence in and through their prophetic commitment would help these religious to experience the God who desires fullness of life for all his creatures. As Schillebeeckx puts it: 'Christian salvation also comprises ecological, social and political aspects, though it is not exhausted by these. Christian salvation is more than that, but it is that, too.'[9]

In a similar way, those who have developed a more creation-centred, mystical approach to their religious life have a great treasure to share with their prophetic brothers and sisters. Their deep sense of union with God, of the presence of God in everything that exists, makes it clear that 'experience of God – call it mysticism, without thereby meaning extraordinary things – is the heart of all human salvation'.[10] At the same time, an equally profound encounter with the prophetic aspects of religious life will help their mysticism to stay rooted, to remain the ordinary mysticism to which all Christians are called by God.

One of the implications of this approach to contemplation and action that is attractive to me as a Salesian of Don Bosco is that the two are not paired in such a way that one is active and the other passive. Though there are spiritual traditions which speak of contemplation as a passive moment in prayer, in which God alone acts, this seems not to be the case in the Dominican tradition from what Schillebeeckx says. Neither is this the way things are seen in my own Salesian tradition. Two examples suggest themselves, the first of which is a story told in Salesian circles about the process of Don Bosco's canonisation. Given how hard he worked, the long hours he and his Salesians spent with the boys in the Oratory, the question arose: 'When did he

---

9. Edward Schillebeeckx, *God Among Us: The Gospel Proclaimed,* (London: SCM Press, 1983), p 100.
10. Edward Schillebeeckx, *Interim Report on the Books: Jesus and Christ,* (London: SCM Press, 1980), p 122.

pray?' 'When did he *not* pray?', came the reply, pointing out the many ways in which, in the midst of his activities, he turned his mind to God and taught others to do the same. When speaking quietly with a boy in recreation who was experiencing difficulties, he would often pray with him, in a simple and undemonstrative way. His conversations with his fellow Salesians would frequently contain short expressions of trust in God and in his providence – especially when there were bills to be paid!

The second example can act as a counterpoint to the story, since it is a reflection on the attitude of prayer itself. The current Rector Major of the Salesians, Pascual Chávez Villanueva, in a letter to the congregation, points out that the most important element of meditative prayer is indeed to be silent and listen to God. However, he also stresses that this attitude of listening is not one 'without either activity or meaning'. It 'must be a reverent and welcoming silence [...] an active silence'.[11] In this way, contemplation could be appropriately described as an active listening to the Creator God, in whose absolute presence we live our lives. Prayer, in this form, is a practice of attention, of attentiveness, an attitude of receptiveness to God's sustaining presence. As such, even if it is most clearly practiced in silent meditation, the attitude that contemplation teaches can be practised in the workplace, the home and the playground, as well as in the chapel. At all times and in all places, we are called to listen for the voice of God who invites us to make a better future for our world.

When Schillebeeckx speaks of the task of making a better future, he describes it in a typically dialectical fashion. He places a critically negative strand alongside a strand that I would call critically optimistic. On the one hand, he extends the idea of suffering as a negative contrast experience (one of the hallmarks of his theology) so as to speak of 'ecological experiences of contrast' that became all too obvious in the twentieth century. These disastrous events and situations, many of which humanity bears responsibility for, have helped believers to widen their sphere of concern beyond the human family. It is true that God is a God

---

11. Pascual Chávez Villanueva, 'The Word of God and Salesian Life Today', *Acts of the General Council of the Salesian Society of St John Bosco*, 386 (Year LXXXV, July-September 2004), 3-52, p 23.

of humanity, a God who is for humanity, but it is also true that this does not give men and women *carte blanche* to do as we will with the planet. Christian faith leads us further, helping us to appreciate that God wants fullness of life for all that God has created. On the basis of this critically negative aspect, he calls for 'self-restraint and a more sober lifestyle in order to protect creation.'[12]

On the other hand, he adds, the lifestyle that God is calling us to 'is not as pessimistic as it seems'. In fact, in addition to this challenging dimension, it has an encouraging one that goes alongside it. There is 'something of a festal element' about it, which can lead to 'a more contemplative and lucid relationship to the world of animals and nature'.[13] In this expression, the pairing of contemplation and action appears again, this time with a relational term in the place of action that means spontaneous or playful. This is the critical optimism of Schillebeeckx's creation -faith, which strikes a resonant chord with me as a Salesian. In the preventive system that guides all Salesian apostolic activity, reference is frequently made to the 'Oratory criterion', against which all our works are to be measured. This criterion has four aspects, all of which should be present in any Salesian work. Don Bosco strove to make his Oratory in Turin a home, in which the boys with whom he worked could be safe and experience it as a place of their own; a school, in which they could learn, grow and develop their talents; a church, in which they could find meaning and a personal relationship with Christ; and a playground, in which they could enjoy themselves and develop their sense of being alongside others in solidarity.[14] The playground criterion was extremely important – whenever anyone coming to work with the young would ask Don Bosco what the best way to get to know them was, he would encourage them to stand by the water tap in the playground, saying that this was the best place to meet them. This presence with the young in recreation is a

---

12. Schillebeeckx, *Church*, p 238.
13. Ibid, p 240.
14. *'Few Words and a Lot of Action ...'*: *an Introduction to the Working Style of Don Bosco Youth-Net ivzw* (Heverleee: Don Bosco Youth-Net ivzw, no date), http://www.donboscoyouth.net/system/files/ Few+words+ and+a+lot+of+action.pdf (Accessed 26 August 2010) pp 14-15.

key element of the preventive system. It is an attentive, friendly presence that shows the young, in a very tangible and practical way, that they are important to the Salesian. As Don Bosco put it: 'It is not enough that young people are loved. They must know that they are loved.'

To sum up, presence can serve as a hermeneutic for a religious life in the midst of creation. It can speak to us of the presence of God in all things, which we pay attention to both in our contemplative prayer and our apostolic activity. This attentiveness helps us to hear, ever more clearly, the voice of God, calling us to relate in ways that are life-giving and life-enriching. God calls us to live a life made in God's image, in which our being and doing are dynamically interlinked. In this kind of life, our actions will spring from a deepening awareness of who we are and who God calls us to become, as men and women living in relationship with God in the midst of creation. In turn, these actions will help us to conform ever more closely to God's image as they make a better future for our world. The mutual interaction of our being and doing will help us to become what Don Bosco wanted for all the young people entrusted to his care. This involves, on the one hand, journeying together on the way to becoming good Christians, committed to an ever-deeper relationship with God in Christ and to being signs and bearers of God's love to all creation. On the other hand, it helps us to become good citizens, playing an active part in the politics of the societies we live in, witnessing to God's preferential option for the poor. We are also called to be citizens of the planet, to be people who are a hopeful presence in the world (even an optimistic one), playfully inviting others to join us in making a future in which the fruits of creation are sustainably shared for the benefit of all.

Reflection questions
1. The author describes mystical/contemplative and prophetic approaches to climate change and biodiversity loss facing the planet. What has been your experience of these different approaches?
2. The divergence in these two approaches is described as creating tension between different religious. How does the critical optimism of Schillebeeckx's creation-faith help to resolve this tension?

4

'Nothing was taken from me: everything was given': Religious Life and Second Wave Feminism

Kate Stogdon RC

Fiat   (Luke 1:38)
I uttered myself
I claimed my voice
I was not afraid to question

I held my ground
I made my yes
Looking straight into the angel's eyes
(any slave girl could have been beaten or raped for less)

There was no mastery here
Nothing was taken from me
Everything was given

Here I am:
See me
Listen.[1]

In Nicola Slee's *Fiat*, a thought-provoking feminist articulation of the words spoken by Mary of Nazareth at the Annunciation, we are brought face to face with the challenge of self-possession and dispossession. Head up, voice clear she gives her 'Yes' to all that will come to be. This is not a passive, resigned consent to her undoing but a courageous choice to trust herself to the divine purpose: 'Here am I, the servant of the Lord; let it be with me according to your word.' (Lk 1:38). At the heart of every vocation to religious life is this invitation to receive the gift of God and the daring decision to acquiesce to its consequences. This essay will consider the impact of the relationship between feminism and religious life and whether it is friend or foe to those striving to live religious vows in the twenty-first century. Which voices

---

1. Taken from Nicola Slee, *The Book of Mary* (London: SPCK, 2007), p. 19 by permission of SPCK.

should we be listening to in analyses of the interaction of feminist values and religious life? Is feminism a symptom of a deeper malaise within society, reflecting the secularising tendency critiqued by Benedict XVI? Or is it necessary to engage with feminist theological thinking in its desire to 'promote the full humanity of women'?[2] Tina Beattie's contention illustrates well what is at stake:

> If male and female are both made in the image of God (Gen 1:27), then the human understanding of God requires the theological participation of both sexes. To bring women's perspectives into theology is not simply to 'add women and stir' but to introduce a catalyst capable of initiating radical transformation.[3]

It will be argued that by paying attention to a middle way between polarising tendencies towards ultra-conservatism and ultra-liberalism the compatibility of feminist commitments and the vocation to religious life may be discerned.

Visitations, misinterpretations and quarrelling hermeneutics
'We have seen it all before' remarks Francine Cardman wryly in her analysis of the apostolic visitation of religious sisters in North America during the course of 2010, locating it within the lengthy process of 'reception' of the teaching of Vatican II. The 'unsettled questions' about interpretation continue to rear their head and witness to a widening chasm it would seem between divergent liberal and conservative approaches to the conciliar legacy.[4] At the heart of the matter for Pope Benedict XVI is the effect of rapid change and secularisation on both society and church. In his pastoral letter to the Catholics of Ireland in March 2010 he laments the negative impact of such 'fast-paced social change' on 'traditional adherence to Catholic teaching and values'. Benedict criticises a 'tendency' of priests and religious 'to adopt

---

2. Rosemary Radford Ruether, *Sexism and God-Talk: Towards a Feminist Theology*, (London, SCM, 1983), p19.
3. Tina Beattie, 'Feminist Theology: Christian Feminist Theology' in L. Jones, ed, *Encyclopaedia of Religion*, (London, Macmillan, 2005), pp 3034-3039, (3035).
4. Francine Cardman, 'Vatican II Revisited', *America*, 4-11 January 2010, pp 11-14, (11-12).

ways of thinking and assessing secular realities without sufficient reference to the gospel', caused by a misinterpretation of the proposed renewal of the Second Vatican Council.[5] This assessment of the secularising influences on the life of the church echoes earlier analysis found in the Pope's Christmas Address of 2005 where he insists on a 'correct interpretation' or 'proper hermeneutics' of the council. Benedict paints an evocative picture of two quarrelling hermeneutics, one of which causes 'confusion' and the other which is increasingly 'bearing fruit':

> On the one hand, there is an interpretation that I would call 'a hermeneutic of discontinuity and rupture'; it has frequently availed itself of the sympathies of the mass media, and also one trend of modern theology. On the other, there is the 'hermeneutic of reform', of renewal in the continuity of the one subject-church which the Lord has given to us. She is a subject which increases in time and develops, yet always remaining the same, the one subject of the journeying People of God.[6]

This 'hermeneutic of discontinuity', he argues, threatens to create a gulf between the pre- and post-conciliar church by its assertion that 'the texts of the Council as such do not yet express the true spirit of the Council.' It is instructive to note how this 'quarrel' exhibits itself within religious life, and the particular tinder box of feminism, which ignites discussions with remarkable ferocity.

The perceived influence of feminism

Cardinal Rodé (formerly prefect of the Congregation for Institutes of Consecrated Life and Societies of Apostolic Life) has used Pope Benedict's critique to devastating effect in his address to the Stonehill symposium in September 2008. In his

5. Benedict XVI, 'Pastoral Letter to the Catholics of Ireland', 4 March 2010, [http://www.vatican.va/holy_father/benedict_xvi/letters/ 2010/ documents/hf_ben-xvi_let_20100319_church-ireland_en.html accessed 3 April 2010]

6. Benedict XVI, 'Christmas Greetings to Curia', December 2005 [http://www.vatican.va/holy_father/benedict_xvi/speeches/2005/d ecember/documents/hf_ben_xvi_spe_20051222_roman-curia_en.html accessed 3 April 2010].

address 'Reforming Religious Life with the Right Hermeneutic' Rodé applies this notion of warring hermeneutics to the contemporary state of religious life. While he affirms those 'new communities' and older communities 'that have taken action to preserve and reform genuine religious life' (noting that these are 'thriving') Rodé's address makes for uncomfortable reading for other religious. While many may identify themselves with his description of those who 'fervently believe in their own personal vocation and the charism of their community' and who want to 'achieve authentic renewal' (whom he wants to encourage) they may not agree so readily to his description of them as wanting to 'reverse the trend' of the decades since Vatican II. It can cause consternation that the majority of women religious are cast into two derogatory groupings: those who have acquiesced peacefully in the decline and disappearance of religious life and those 'who have opted for ways that take them outside communion with Christ in the Catholic Church, although they themselves may have opted to "stay" in the church physically.'[7] Drawing on Pope Benedict's secularisation motif, Rodé highlights what is seen as the source of such developments within religious life:

> We cannot ignore that some concrete choices [of consecrated life] have not offered to the world the authentic and vivifying face of Christ. In fact, the secularised culture has penetrated the mind and heart of not a few consecrated persons, who understand it as a way to enter modernity and a modality of approach to the contemporary world ... Consecrated life today knows the temptation to mediocrity, bourgeois ways and a consumerist mentality.[8]

This interpretation of religious in general is particularised through the identification of the distinct problem of women

---

7 Cardinal Franc Rodé, 'Reforming Religious Life with the Right Hermeneutic', 4-5, September 2008 [http://www.stonehill.edu/x14963.xml accessed 3 April 2010].

8. Benedict XVI, 'Address to Superiors General of the Institutes of Consecrated Life and Societies of Apostolic Life', 10, May 22, 2006, (quoted by Rodé). http://www.vatican.va/holy_father/benedict_xvi/speeches/2006/may/documents/hf_ben-xvi_spe_20060522_vita-consacrata_en.html accessed 3 April 2010].

religious and their appropriation of feminist principles. In paragraph 15 Rodé appeals to the more conservative among them to contest this influence: 'Women religious especially need to engage critically *a certain strain of feminism by now outmoded* but which still nevertheless continues to exert much influence in certain circles' (my emphasis). Sr Sara Butler, a Missionary Servant of the Most Blessed Trinity, who teaches dogmatic theology at St Joseph's Seminary, New York and was appointed to the International Theological Commission in 2004 was a keynote speaker at Stonehill and is also critical of the influence of feminism on religious life since Vatican II. Butler analyses the period of adaptation and renewal following the council, and the 'competing ecclesiologies … theological pluralism and public dissent' within the church.[9] She describes 'many women religious' as 'caught up in the feminist movement' and therefore claiming 'the right to self-determination as regards the future of their own institutes'(13). In her critique of the role of religious in protesting injustices in society and within the church (highlighting the issues of contraception, abortion, mandatory clerical celibacy and ordination of women to the priesthood, divorce and remarriage, gay and lesbian rights), Butler emphasises the contribution of 'leading feminist theologians' in the promotion of this agenda for change (14-15). She cites in particular Schneiders's description of the 'feminist project' in *Finding the Treasure* as 'the dismantling of the patriarchal system of domination and subordination that structures the institutional church and its replacement by a system of gospel equality, justice and love'.[10]

Butler describes in stark battle lines the polarisation between a 'hierarchically-structured church' versus the 'discipleship of equals' as articulated by Elisabeth Schüssler Fiorenza.[11] On the one side stand those '"Conservatives" who accept the church's

---

9 Butler, Sarah, 'Apostolic Religious Life: a Public, Ecclesial Vocation' September 2008 [http://www.stonehill.edu/x14963.xml accessed 3 April 2010]
10. Sandra M. Schneiders, *Finding the Treasure*, (New York, Paulist Press, 2000), p 35, quoted in Butler p 15.
11. Elisabeth Schüssler Fiorenza, *Discipleship of Equals: a Critical Feminist Ekklesialogy of Liberation*, (New York Crossroad, 1993).

hierarchical structure, teaching authority, and jurisdiction; they are eager to collaborate with the bishops, gain their approval, and be publicly associated with them' (16). On the other are grouped the 'liberals' (or perhaps, the 'radicals') who distinguish between the church as the 'people of God' (which they profess to love) and the 'institutional church (from which they feel alienated)'. They are wary of distinctions based on sex or status or power, and they long for the day when all 'dualistic hierarchies' are brought down and replaced by a 'discipleship of equals'.[12]

In this battle for the hearts and minds of religious, Butler is unequivocal about where the truth is located, describing the model of church outlined by Schüssler Fiorenza as 'incompatible with Catholic doctrine' and arguing that 'radical feminism' forms the ideological foundation of such anti-hierarchical definitions. She spells out the consequences of a 'discipleship of equals ecclesiology' stating *it must be said forthrightly that those who reject the God-given authority of the hierarchy … simply cut the ground out from under the vocation to "religious life" as the church understands and regulates it'* (19 emphasis in original). Butler contends that in practice notions of a 'discipleship of equals' base community on 'a doctrine of equal rights' rather than on 'a response of self-emptying love'. Dialogue and consensus are more likely, she argues, to lead to a greater 'independent living' than to 'common life' (20). According to Butler, 'traditional' religious 'stand as witnesses against their liberal sisters and brothers in religion' and the 'silent majority … 'remain aloof from the dispute' … 'deeply immersed in their ministry and feel no responsibility for the state of religious life as a whole' (18).

This powerful indictment of the majority of religious and the toxic influence of feminism could be a manifestation of a 'defensive authoritarianism' such as described by Tina Beattie in her description of the then Cardinal Ratzinger's reductionist attitude towards feminism in 2004 in his 'Collaboration of Men and Women in the Church'. Beattie identifies in this letter an attack on feminism as a whole, without any recognition of the plurality of perspectives that is contained within it. The authority of the Catholic hierarchy is set up over against 'antagonistic' and

---

12. Ibid, pp 184-7 quoted in Butler p 17.

'adversarial' feminism which is evidently 'to blame for the animosity between the sexes'.[13] The antipathy expressed towards feminism as symptomatic of a greater disorder within religious congregations during the Stonehill symposium would seem to support such a thesis.

Feminisms, for good or ill

Feminism is a slippery term, which mostly seems to evoke a strong reaction and to get 'frozen' into a stereotypical negative association with 1960s' debunking of institutional strictures. Mentioning it conjures up images of Germaine Greer alongside Beatlemania. Popular connotations of radical feminists clad in dungarees appear to haunt those seeking to describe their commitment to women's equality as they protest 'I'm not a feminist but ... I do believe that women have a lot to contribute to society and to the life of the church today' and so on. This testifies to social and cultural assumptions about the significant roles played by women within church and society and the presumption of equality of opportunity, access to education and fair wages. Such a disassociation may be akin to the religious/spiritual descriptors utilised by those who protest: 'I'm not religious but ...' as they articulate their rejection of religious institutions in favour of a more eclectic embracing of a generic 'spirituality' with diverse faces.

First wave feminism, then (of the late nineteenth and early twentieth century) did indeed stress notions of the equality of women with men, resting on a liberal ideology culminating in the achievement of suffrage in the early decades of the century. Second wave feminism (following the publication in 1949 of Simone de Beauvoir's *The Second Sex*) shifted attention to women's difference or particularity and took shape in the context of 1960s struggles for civil rights and the anti-war movement, particularly in the United States. What both waves had in common was bringing to the fore the category of 'woman' as the centre (or subject) of enquiry rather than as object. In her outline of feminist thinking within society and church, Schneiders sketches the main phases and positions within the field. Her presentation of

---

13. Tina Beattie, *New Catholic Feminism: Theology and Theory*, (London, Routledge, 2006), pp 20-23.

liberal, cultural, socialist and radical models of feminism illustrates the impact of social and political context in the formulation and living out of feminist ideals (18-25).[14] It is important to note the tension that exists between those who want to emphasise 'sameness' (equality) and those who insist on 'difference' (particularity). This has resulted in debates about the best way to value women's humanity whether it is through an insistence on equal rights and opportunities or instead their femaleness, which is not equitable to maleness and should be valued in itself as different. This can make for strange bedfellows so that both radical feminists and the Vatican insist on the particularity of women's nature.

Within feminist theology two central themes have been to promote the full humanity of women as theological subjects (Ruether's 'critical principle') and the determination to uncover and listen to 'women's experience' within history, theology and spirituality.[15] The value of autonomy has prevailed but the universalising, liberal tendency of early second wave feminism to talk about 'woman' as a unitary, self-governing subject has been challenged in consequent waves of feminist scholarship informed by a variety of social, political, economic, religious and cultural factors. This has resulted in a range of feminist perspectives within theology, contributing new insights to how we understand: God, biblical interpretation, christology, anthropology, ecclesiology, moral theology, spirituality and so on.[16]

In her revised edition of *Beyond Patching*, Schneiders spells out what she understands by 'gospel feminism' which was given public expression in the *Madaleva Manifesto*, 29 April 2000. 'It consists in the explicit recognition by feminist Catholics that what they are talking about and promoting is not a baptised version of secular feminism but "evangelical" or "gospel feminism" (xv).' Schneiders argues that this manifesto comes from

14. Sandra M. Schneiders, *Beyond Patching: Faith and Feminism in the Catholic Church,* (revised edition, New York, Paulist Press, 2004).
15. Ruether, *Sexism and God-Talk*, pp 18-19.
16. Catherine Mowry Lacugna, ed, *Freeing Theology: the Essentials of Theology in Feminist Perspective* (New York, Harper Collins, 1993) and Anne M. Clifford, *Introducing Feminist Theology,* (New York, Orbis, 2001).

women who 'have remained faithful participants in the church while becoming ever more committed feminists' and reflects their beliefs that they are not trying to achieve within the church what feminists in general are trying to achieve for women in society. 'They are claiming as their own the agenda of Jesus in the gospel, what he called "the coming of the reign of God," and insisting that feminist commitment is not just compatible with but is integral to commitment to the gospel.' For Schneiders then 'the feminist message itself is a contemporary incarnation of the gospel' (xv-xvi).

Autonomy and heteronomy

For the purposes of this essay I want to focus on feminist theological discussions about autonomy and heteronomy because the making of religious vows (so crucial to the identity of religious) can appear incongruent with feminist commitments to freedom and self-determination. Is the base line within feminism about autonomy, human rights, self-empowerment and equality of access or is this a reductionist reading of feminist concerns? Ursula King argues that:

> The modern women's movement, especially in its contemporary feminist phase, gives expression to women's active determination to shape their own 'self' and the world around them. Instead of passively conforming to a predetermined role, women want to actively decide for themselves what to be and do, and what to contribute to the life of society.[17]

This echoes of course that quest, epitomized by Virginia Woolf in *A Room of One's Own*, the determination to exercise a sense of agency. It should be noted, however, that feminist theory (like feminist theology) also grapples with a variety of viewpoints on the relative values of community and autonomy within feminist ideals.[18] The principle of self-agency is taken to its extreme in

---

17. Ursula King, *Women and Spirituality: Voices of Protest and Promise*, (London, MacMillan, 1989), pp 1-2.
18. Catriona Mackenzie and Natalie Stoljar, eds, *Relational Autonomy: Feminist Perspectives on Autonomy, Agency and the Social Self*, (Oxford, OUP, 2000).

the work of feminist thinkers like Daphne Hampson (who now identifies herself as post-Christian) in her assertion that 'Feminists … believe in autonomy.' In her contributions to a feminist theological debate on the credibility of Christianity, Hampson insists on the necessity of feminists to be self-ruling rather than to subject themselves to the law of another (a situation of heteronomy). By centring themselves in God, she argues, Christians necessarily undermine themselves, not daring to follow Kant's admonition to use their own understanding and knowledge.[19] Rosemary Radford Ruether has sought to overcome the polarity between ideas of autonomy and dependency by advancing a theory of power expressed in her description of the kenosis of patriarchy, or the 'self-emptying of power as domination'. To exercise power as a means of liberation rather than domination challenges patriarchal constructions of power. 'Service to others does not deplete the person who ministers' she contends 'but rather causes her (or him) to become more liberated'.[20] Hampson is not convinced, maintaining that self-emptying and self-abnegation have no place alongside feminist principles of self-actualisation and equality.[21]

Sarah Coakley, however, counter-challenges this critique of Ruether's use of *kenosis*, arguing that Hampson makes female autonomy a supreme good and reduces the notion of *kenosis* to only 'self-destructive subordination' for women. In contrast, she distinguishes what she calls a 'right' *kenosis* or 'power-in vulnerability', grounding this in the practice of contemplative prayer, where a 'special form of vulnerability or self-effacement' and 'personal empowerment' are held together in the space where a 'non-coercive divine power' manifests itself.[22] Lamenting what she called the 'repression of all forms of vulnerability'

---

19. Daphne Hampson, 'On Autonomy and Heteronomy', in D. Hampson, ed, *Swallowing a Fishbone? Feminist Theologians Debate Christianity,* (London, SPCK, 1996), pp 1–16, (1).
20. Ruether, *Sexism and God-Talk*, pp 137-8, 207.
21. Daphne Hampson, *Theology and Feminism*, (Oxford, Blackwell, 1990), pp 153-5.
22. Sarah Coakley, '*Kenosis* and Subversion', in D. Hampson, ed, *Swallowing a Fishbone? Feminist Theologians Debate Christianity,* (London, SPCK,1996), pp 82 –111 (84).

within Christian feminism (except in terms of victimology) Coakley calls for a feminist re-reading of the power of the dynamic of the cross and resurrection. She describes how, through the practice of silent 'waiting on ... ceding and responding to the divine', the self makes 'space', leading not to self-loss and silencing of the self but rather to its 'transformation and expansion into God'(106-8). Coakley points out the unease in the affluent West with any idea of submission, opposed so neatly to the quest for autonomy or agency. 'Surrender' she has charged 'is seemingly at the cost of "freedom" (so understood), a delimitation of options, a clamp on the desire for delicious risk-taking possibilities'. This stems, she argues, from a cultural fear of 'heteronomy – of submission, dependency or vulnerability'. The choice between 'dependent vulnerability' and 'liberative power' however is a false one.[23]

Beattie also considers the role of contemplation within Christian feminism. She describes an 'unfolding' to be found through 'the mysterious encounter between the unknown self and the incomprehensible God, an encounter that comes about through love and desire, and sometimes through darkness and chaos – not through power and control.' 'It is a process' she states, 'in which the self, God and creation are caught up in the mystery of being'.[24] How can women, Beattie asks, while preserving their 'fragile sense of self' acquired through modernity, discover a way to 'willingly abandon ourselves to God in the confidence that this God is an Other who participates in our personal becoming and makes us *more* rather than *less* the selves we seek to be' (my emphasis)? Beattie emphasises the need to locate 'women's religious desire' in 'particular contexts', translated into the 'grammar and practices of faith communities'. I want to underline here the concrete nature of this picture of the desiring, contemplative woman:

> It is in knowing who a woman prays to, how she prays, why she prays, who she prays with, and how this in turn shapes

---

23. Sarah Coakley, *Powers and Submissions: Spirituality, Philosophy and Gender*, (Oxford, Blackwell, 2002), pp xii-xx.
24. Beattie, *New Catholic Feminism*, p 64.

her understanding of who she is, that we might begin to understand the significance of desire for feminist reflection.[25]

A reconciling middle way?

Feminist discussions about autonomy and heteronomy give an entry point to considering the impact of feminism on religious life that does not necessarily re-inscribe polarised divisions into ultra-conservative or ultra-liberal factions within the church. A more considered reading of feminist conversations about the need to have an adequate enough sense of self before one is able freely to give it away altruistically or spiritually (and without damaging self or others) shows that the resulting strong sense of self is not the end of the story.[26] The robust selfhood captured so well in Slee's 'nothing was taken from me ... everything was given' portrays a critical dimension of Mary's 'Yes' and yet there is more, which she learns over the course of a lifetime. The giving of oneself in love to the purposes of God is precisely about the assent to an ongoing transformation through a radical availability to the divine initiative. Religious vows illustrate that in a particular, stark and iconic way through the public, visible following of Christ, chaste, poor and obedient. It is important to recognise the deepening conversion that occurs through the 'life form devoted to the single hearted quest for God through union with Christ' that is religious life.[27] So-called 'traditional' expressions of religious life do not have the monopoly on what 'total dedication, perfection of charity, building up the life of the church' ... 'oblation' ... 'sacrifice' ... 'availability' look like.[28]

How can contemporary religious life (in all its divergent manifestations) be made more visible and accessible? How does

---

25. Ibid, pp 73, 78.

26. Katharine M. Stogdon, 'The Risk of Surrender: *Se Livrer* in the Life of Thérèse Couderc (1805-1885)', Ph.D. thesis, University of Manchester, 2004.

27. Sandra M. Schneiders, *Selling All*, (New York, Paulist Press, 2001), p 158.

28. Agnes Mary Donovan, Mary Elizabeth Wusinich 'Religious Consecration - A Particular Form of Consecrated Life' in Council of Major Religious Superiors of Women Religious,ed., *The Foundations of Religious Life: Revisiting the Vision*, (Notre Dame, Ave Maria, 2009) pp 14-45 (20-27)

religious life witness to the values at its heart and give an account of the hope that is found within it? Articulating some responses to Beattie's questions would be a beginning. 'Who do we pray to? How do we pray? Why do we pray? Who do we pray with? How does this shape our understanding of who we are?' Our answers would lay bare the meaning of this way of life and its necessary rootedness in the Jesus Christ of the gospels. Any form of religious life should be charismatic (Spirit led), public (not private, individual), ecclesial (of necessity in relation, accountable, discerning), visible (capable of being seen and recognised), stable or mobile (in service of the gospel), in relation to the world (incarnational, counter-cultural), vowed (poor, chaste, obedient, following in relationship to Christ), sacrificial (gift) and an experience of oblation (transformation). None of these elements seem to me to be in contradiction to feminist ideals. In the forms of religious life lived in the twenty-first century there is a growing appreciation of the power of symbolic as well as physical space in which life lived in communion is made tangible and available to succeeding generations. The utopian hope embodied in the vowed life needs to be offered anew in such a way that it makes sense in the contexts in which it is currently lived out. The counter-cultural commitment of all that is held most dear in service of this gospel vision engenders life in all its fullness. Yet how will people experience this reality of love shared and given, hope in the midst of diminishment, freedom in the face of fear, gift arising from loss unless we tell them?

Where does this leave feminism?

Anna (not her real name), a woman in her early thirties considering Religious Life shared the following response to the topic of feminism and religious life:

> I have only ever looked at feminism in a very superficial way … and I had to google 'second wave feminism' to see what it is. I am sure there must be a middle way. Keep looking! We cannot turn the clock back and I am sure that modern women must be able to find a way of living lives dedicated to God without completely destroying their identity as modern women. I have vaguely been aware of church dislike of feminism but assumed it was being used euphemistically of

lesbians. If it is just feminism in the sense of women recognising themselves as valuable and capable human beings, then people are being foolish.

We cannot ignore the role and effects of feminist thinking within both society and church. Feminist critiques arose out of the historical struggles of the nineteenth and twentieth centuries and have contributed to twenty-first-century assumptions about what it means to be human. We cannot bypass these, anymore than we can ignore the questions posed by atheism. Neither, however, is it helpful to collude with the polarising split into conservative/liberal extremes. There must be a middle way because we surely need it. The vast majority of people in the West take for granted progress made in society (for example, suffrage, access to the workplace) and eschew feminist labels. Yet, discrimination and inequality continue as realities both at home and on the international stage where poverty, war, violence, sex trafficking and so on, still disproportionately affect women and stop them from reaching their truly human potential.

Do feminist values expressed in and through the religious life form give it any added value? Maybe that is the wrong question and instead we should acknowledge the authenticity of such developments as part of the diverse life of the church. Not one that has the last word, but which can be discerned as one pathway of the Holy Spirit in our time. In fact it is very important not to lose the variety of ways of what it means to be a religious in today's postmodern, globalised world. Feminist religious (as 'other') give expression to what religious life looks like from a particular standpoint. This generates a 'situated knowledge' that is vital to discern the future direction of conse- crated life. It is a valid exemplar of a charismatic lifeform with a long and varied history, according to historical contexts. In her consideration of female apostolic religious life Cardman warns us not to 'buy (or slip) into the false dichotomies of "traditional" and "non-traditional" religious life'.[29] Members of the Leadership Conference of Women Religious (representing 95 per cent of US sisters) she argues 'have legitimate claims to

29. Cardman, *Vatican II Revisited*, p 13

stand in the long and diverse tradition of authentic, apostolic communities of women religious' (13). Cardman underlies two features in current struggles over what constitutes 'tradition' and legitimate 'change', which have long been a part of the history of women's religious life. Firstly she notes the 'creativity, persistence and patience' exercised by women religious as they have 'sought ways of life to express their commitment to the gospel in changing historical circumstances'. Secondly, she makes explicit the 'resistance' encountered by such groups as they sought ecclesiastical approval of their charisms. She concludes by underlining the need for 'many expressions of apostolic religious life' if the church is to be truly catholic and missionary (14). Feminist influences on the development of ways of living religious life should not be reduced to simply subversion of the hierarchical church. They may yet stand the test of time.

Reflection questions

1. Quoting arguments from the Stonehill Symposium the author speaks of a contrast drawn between different forms of feminism which lead to incompatible views of discipleship. What do you understand these to be? How do you experience these differing views of discipleship?

2. Daphne Hampson and Sarah Coakley are quoted as having opposed views on *kenosis* (self-emptying love). How do you see these, and how do they connect with the vows of religious life?

3. What is the 'reconciling middle way' of feminism proposed by the author? How do you perceive it as a way of interpreting religious life for women?

PART TWO

The Once and Future Vocation

Compass in the Catholic Church: Finding a Path to Vocation Discernment

Christopher Jamison OSB

Vocations are not where they used to be

Br Robert Verrill OP became a Dominican novice in 2006; in an online account of his vocational journey, he describes his state of mind in 2004 when he was a software engineer in his mid-twenties.'Although my feelings on religious life were ambiguous, I felt I really needed to talk to someone, but I had no idea who to turn to. I didn't want to speak to my parish priest. I felt that if I spoke to him, the next thing I'd know, I'd be before the bishop being asked to sign on the dotted line. Where was I to turn? Well, I turned to Google.'

Contrast this with Archbishop Vincent Nichols' vocation story as he recently told it to an audience of young people considering their vocation. He described how as a fifteen-year-old school boy he went to see his parish priest because the young Vincent thought that God wanted him to be a priest. The differences between these two stories about responding to the call of Christ tell us much about how vocation responses have changed within a generation. The difference is not only in the responses but also in the media through which the two stories are recounted, the medium being as significant as the story. The call of Christ is constant but the way people respond and the media they use to describe their responses have changed beyond recognition.

The path referred to in the title of this essay is not the path of the person seeking to discern their vocation. The path to which this essay refers is the path to be pursued by congregations and clergy who wish to foster vocations to the religious life and priesthood. Some religious and clergy operate, albeit uncon-sciously, with a working assumption that since the old and well worn path to the seminary or novitiate has collapsed, there is no longer any realistic way to foster vocations. They know in theory that some people somewhere are still joining but not at a novitiate or seminary near them. Some priests have stopped learning about new opportunities to foster religious or priestly vocations. Some religious now say that their charism will be carried on by lay associates in Europe and by new recruits in developing countries. At a meeting about new approaches to vocations ministry, I recently met a religious who insisted that her sizeable congregation had nobody available to undertake this new work. She explained that with declining numbers nobody could be spared from their important ministries. The emerging new approach to vocations ministry under discussion at the meeting would have meant reorienting at least part of the congregation and this seemed a leap of the imagination that she was unable to make.

Most religious and clergy who embraced change in so many areas of the church's life in the 70s and 80s did not change their attitude to vocations work. Formation programmes changed dramatically but assumptions about the stage before that remained unchanged. The assumption was that there still existed, albeit now in much smaller numbers, a well formed, youthful laity from stable Catholic homes and/or Catholic schools and/or active parishes who thought about priestly and religious vocation as part of their upbringing. On this model, vocations directors simply meet with well formed people who want information about which orders or seminaries to consider. This can be described as skimming the cream off the top of the solidly nourished Catholic milk. The contemporary reality is that the Catholic milk has evaporated and there is no creaming off to be done. This is not the place to discuss why this has happened but recognition of its effect is crucial to a person's ability to foster future vocations to the religious and priestly life.

The apostolic religious congregations of the 70s and 80s and many monastic orders set about renewing their lives to become what some would call more modern. The steps of that renewal included engagement with issues of social justice, a lifestyle that was considered more contemporary, methods of governance that were more participatory and decentralised. For women's congregations, contemporary feminism was a strong influence. The assumption regarding recruitment was that young

Catholics would be more likely to join communities renewed in this way. There were just sufficient people still joining in some places for this to be a valid strategy for that time. So now instead of vocations promoters, the attraction of modern religious life itself would draw people to join. Underneath this new attitude, however, there was no shift away from the 'creaming off the top' model. So as recruitment dried up in the 90s neither established religious congregations nor diocesan vocations directors understood what was happening or knew what to do.

The people with the answers seemed to be the new movements who were recruiting more strongly than ever. Many combined a lay membership with a religious congregation under a common umbrella. For example, in North America, the Legionaries of Christ with their lay association *Regnum Christi*; in France, the Community of St Jean with contemplative sisters, apostolic sisters and priests, all accompanied by lay associates. What disconcerts the older congregations is that these new movements, while having many modern elements, emphasise Catholic orthodoxy, absolute obedience to the Pope and 'traditional' devotions such as adoration of the Blessed Sacrament. This is a different direction from that undertaken by many religious congregations in the previous forty years. So the idea that a modern style of religious life would of itself attract young people was now being challenged.

The approach of the new movements has not been universally successful, however, as seen by the major crises that have affected many such movements: after thirty years of apparent flourishing, the *Pain de Vie* community in France has collapsed into acrimony, including a successful law suit against the founder; in Italy an Apostolic Visitation removed the founding abbot of the monastic *Fraternitá di Gesú*; most astonishingly, the Holy See has taken control of the Legionaries of Christ following startling revelations about their founder. So the belief that the new movements have all the answers to religious life and priesthood in the twenty-first century is not self-evident. This belief is, however, often strongly affirmed by the founders of such movements. For example, in his book *A Drama of Reform*,[1] Fr Benedict Groeschel

1. Benedict Groeschel, *A Drama of Reform*, (San Francisco, Ignatius Press, 2005).

of the Franciscan Friars of the Renewal devotes a lengthy section to describing in detail the errors of other religious congregations and how his new congregation will correct them.

What the new movements have certainly grasped, however, is that the underlying model of recruitment has changed. They see that the 'creaming off the top' model has gone and they have consciously replaced it with a new model that sees proclaiming the gospel as the seed bed from which vocations can be grown. This is a complete model of evangelisation, catechesis and discernment, from seed to fully grown vocation. We might call this the 'grow your own vocations' model.

Being the church: ecclesiology in practice
Pope John Paul II was attentive to the changes affecting young people and vocations during the 1990s, so in 1997 he summoned the 'Congress on Vocations to the Priesthood and to Consecrated Life in Europe.' *In Verbo Tuo: New Vocations for a New Europe* was the final statement of that congress in which the church called not only for 'a new vocational culture' but also for 'a new evangelisation.'[2] The new movements responded clearly and quickly to this call for an evangelising approach to vocations. They have a view of the church formed during the pontificate of Pope John Paul and have been very attentive to his ecclesiology. The way they lived out their membership of the church, was aligned with the ecclesiology highlighted by *In Verbo Tuo*: proclamation of the gospel in the name of the Catholic church and a context in which to make a personal response to the call of Christ.

This contrasts with the ecclesiology of the nineteenth and early twentieth century church which was strongly hierarchical and is typically described as a pyramid with the pope at the top. In the 70s and 80s this gave way to a theology of the church derived from an oversimplified reading of *Lumen Gentium*, stating that all are equal in the church. This could be characterised as the ecclesiology of the level playing field. The operative ecclesiology of the church currently embraced by the new movements is neither of these but is experienced by some as a return to the pyramid.

2. See http://www.vatican.va/roman_curia/congregations/ ccatheduc/documents/rc_con_ccatheduc_doc_13021998_new-vocations_en.html

A better description of the contemporary operative ecclesiology, however, would be to describe the church neither as a pyramid nor as a level playing field but as a varied landscape, with different groups within the church occupying diverse hills and valleys. This is best illustrated with regard to liturgy: the Parish Mass of the *Missa Normativa* is still strong, but there is the Extraordinary Form of the liturgy as well, and the Neo-Catechumenate with its special rite; soon there will be another island with the Anglican Rite. This is not a return to an authoritarian one size fits all; it is more subtle than that. Contemporary ecclesiology is centred on active membership of a communion of faith, lived out as active membership of an identifiable group, the fruit of evangelisation by that group.

If we now look at recruitment models in the light of how people actually live in the church, we see that 'creaming off the top' fits the hierarchical model very neatly; the best young men and women simply float to the top. But a model of recruitment to fit the 'level playing field' church is hard to imagine; since we are all the same, what's the point of anybody joining anything other than a local parish or base community. In fact, the 'creaming off the top' model may have subconsciously remained as a recruitment model even as the ecclesiology changed dramatically into the level playing field. This caused recruitment to seize up because the two parts, ecclesiology and recruitment model, were not in harmony.

I believe that the new movements have discovered in their own way a recruitment model that matches the model of church as a varied landscape. They have staked out for themselves a place within that landscape, a very specific response to the call of Christ. Many religious and clergy had great difficulty in understanding the changes happening in the church during the 1990s and did not respond creatively to this work of the Spirit, which led to a vacuum. Into this vacuum the new movements stepped. They all created a clear identity but some were in danger of filling the gap with kitsch, that is, with items that were cheap imitations of the real thing. In the case of those starting new forms of consecrated life, some simply ransacked the past to put together random features that lacked coherence. For example, one group had a pious devotion to St Benedict and St Bernard combined with daily talks on scripture by the founder and they called this 'new monasticism,' with no understanding of the Rule of Benedict or the monastic tradition of *lectio divina*. Among common features of the emerging new forms of consecrated life are obedience to the founder, traditional devotions and externals such as the habit, with the enthusiasm of the founder as the driving force. Their contagious enthusiasm has in some cases proved to be nothing more than enthusiasm or in the worst cases, an expression of a controlling personality, with sad consequences for those who joined in good faith.

The best of the new movements, however, have been important bearers of new life in the church. Some have had difficulty fitting into the local church while others have brought new life to parishes. Those movements that have won official approval are rooted in an intense community life and in fidelity to the church's teaching, these two features combining to create an identity that is both local and universal. This enables members of the movements to have a deeply personal sense of belonging to the church.

So how does the life of the church play out for Catholics aged twenty to forty who have some sense of vocation? In this varied ecclesial landscape, people join the church through a significant encounter with other people of faith. The young in particular are socialised into the church rather than persuaded to join by argument. This social gateway into faith occurs in many different contexts that match the varied landscape of contemporary culture as well as the varied landscape of the church. For some social action will be the opening into faith; for example, membership of a university Life group or participation in a volunteer programme overseas run by a religious order. For others, the path involves a group such as Youth 2000 that offers retreats to young people or other movements that offer a whole way of life, such as the Neo-Catechumenate. In all such groups, web-based networking plays a central role holding together groups both locally and globally. This social gateway into faith through groups and networks always involves an explicitly Catholic identity which is regularly celebrated not only in the Eucharist but also in devotions, pro-life campaigns and events such as World Youth Day.

This leads naturally into the second feature of those who successfully evangelise modern European culture. The group offers catechesis into Catholic faith and sees deeper sacramental life as the goal of catechesis. Social analysis and social action are present but as a means of entering more deeply into the mystical Body of Christ, the church. This catechesis leads into sacramental experience, which in turn brings new energy and a renewed sense of Catholic identity. The desire for a distinctive identity is the key to understanding much of both British and Catholic culture today. There is no longer one British youth culture but a variety of sub-cultures. The features shared by these diverse sub-cultures are their digital means of communication and the music industry that feeds each sub-group. Within this deconstructed world of disparate groups held together electronically, a Catholic needs a Catholic identity. Young Catholics share the media and the music along with all their contemporaries but need to have their own sub-group with which they can identify, a sub-group that then uses the media and the music to reinforce their faith.

This then leads to the third feature of an understanding of the Church that attracts people today, namely, *koinonia*. This New Testament word was first used in Acts of the Apostles to describe the early church and was used in the fourth century to describe the first monastic communities, the forerunners of today's religious congregations. This Greek word is translated into Latin as *communio* and into English as communion. It is worth avoiding the English word 'community' because that word has a debased value that no longer captures the evangelical meaning of *koinonia* or *communio*. The English phrase 'the local community' usually refers to those living in a geographic post code rather than to any human connection between them. *Koinonia* describes a deep union with others, filled with the life of the Spirit, not a physical proximity. Within a religious congregation, this raises issues of control, freedom and life in common, issues that were addressed in the 60s and 70s. Some of the solutions to those issues from that period now look outdated and need to be reconsidered. There is a wide variety of ways of living it but congregations need to choose one way and invite others to join it. Those movements and congregations that live *koinonia* clearly and strongly attract people to join.

The three dimensions just described are those aspects of the church that attract people today. They represent three understandings of the church through which people today progress:

- Evangelisation: people see the social reality of the People of God
- Catechesis: people enter into the sacramental reality of the Body of Christ
- *Koinonia*: people engage deeply with other members of the Body of Christ

All three are needed as an expression of Catholic faith in order to enable people today to respond to the call of Christ, both his call to membership of the church and his call to religious or priestly life.

Compass in the Catholic Church

The analysis offered in the first two parts of this essay has come both from studying the issues and from the experience of addressing the issues in practice. In 2003, concerned by the lack of initiatives in this area, I invited any religious congregations that wished to participate with my own monastic community in an experiment. In faith, we believed that God was still calling people to religious life but our knowledge of contemporary culture lead us to a hunch: young Catholics with an inkling of a religious vocation might not know where to turn for help. We guessed, however, that they might turn to the internet for guidance on this as on everything else in their lives.

Using a powerful website, www.compass-points.org.uk, combined with a Google Adwords campaign and eschewing printed materials, we launched Compass. Compass is a discernment process for Catholic women and men aged twenty to thirty-five who have some sense of a religious vocation and wish to explore this further. The process is residential, led jointly by a male and a female religious, and comprises attending a residential programme for one weekend a month for nine months and for one week at Easter. It began at Worth Abbey in 2004 and is currently expanding to other places in Britain and Ireland. While legal responsibility lies with Worth Abbey, Compass receives financial support from about forty religious congregations and is governed by an Advisory Board comprising religious members of some of those congregations as well as a representative from the English and Welsh Bishops' National Office for Vocation. The Advisory Board appoints and supports the leaders, sets the policy and meets with each group of participants at the end of their time to assess the process.

The programme comprises seven weekends between September and March, then Holy Week, then two more weekends. The programme unfolds a deeper understanding of vocation and an introduction to the nature of religious life and ministry, all set within a shared experience of discernment within the group. The process begins with reflection on each person's life-faith journey before moving into a presentation on the gift of religious life in the church. The nature of vocation is presented through the baptismal vocation and this is the basis for discerning the state of life to which God calls people. So the discernment is rooted in baptism and in greater self-knowledge. From this foundation, the vows are then examined. Holy Week offers an extended period of discernment within the context of the paschal mystery. The penultimate weekend is for evaluation and appreciation; with the final weekend for celebration and moving on. To give the process a practical grounding, a young religious attends some weekends and presents their vocational story. Finally, each participant is connected with a spiritual director near where they live. This whole programme has evolved and been refined over the years, and will continue to evolve.

People come to know about Compass through the web site and, increasingly, through the recommendation of spiritual directors and vocations directors. Compass receives over 100 enquiries a year and many of these are passed on to other places better suited to the enquirers' needs. In the six years since its inauguration, forty-one people have begun the residential process and thirty-one of these completed it. Of those who stayed the course, about half have to date become candidates for a religious order or seminary, with more still considering the possibility.

Keen to offer the same opportunity to those unable to participate because of geographical distance from Worth Abbey, the Compass Board has agreed to support other religious who wish to start other Compass centres. Compass North West has opened in Salford and discussions are also underway to start Compass Ireland.

An unexpected spin off from Compass has been the emergence of an annual study day, started at the suggestion of the Association of British Carmels, one of the project's first supporters. They suggested that Compass participants could give some indication to religious congregations about how religious life needs to evolve to meet the realities of the next generation of religious. It is striking that a community of enclosed women saw this opportunity. The first study day was held in 2006 and since then has become a forum with two dimensions: firstly, Compass participants tell their vocational story, enabling the religious present to engage with a demographic group that they find increasingly hard to contact; secondly, between the religious themselves, there is an increasingly profound dialogue about how promoting vocations is more about the development of religious life itself than about advertising. So what has Compass been teaching congregations about the future of religious life itself?

Firstly, that there is a difference between what is stated by congregations about fostering vocations and what potential candidates experience; religious need to consider carefully their theology of church and whether it encourages new members or unwittingly repels them. Affirming that a congregation renewed itself forty years ago after Vatican II is an inadequate response to this challenge. We now live in a post-Vatican II church in the same sense that we also live in a post-Nicaea I church.

Secondly, Compass is where the three key elements outlined above became clear to those of us privileged to be involved. Through a web site that is designed for the purpose, Compass invites people to be part of a group of like minded Catholics. For some people, this preliminary response to vocation is also a step in their evangelisation. So, for example, they may have only recently returned to the practice of their faith and that return is connected to a sense of vocation. Since Compass is for a limited time and people are offered support rather than an introduction to an order or seminary, they can embrace it as both a deepening of faith and as a step towards discerning vocation. The group then experiences a year of catechesis together, focusing on teaching about vocation and the religious life. This builds a strong sense of *koinonia* so the participants experience a microcosm of the church at its best, male and female, lay and ordained, apostolic and monastic. The participants frequently say that at first they were wary of vocational discernment in a group but by the end they see it as the most helpful way they can imagine. Crucially, this is not communal discernment where each individual's decision is made by the group. Instead, this is personal discernment with the support of the group, a *koinonia* that recognises individuality.

Finally, congregations working together in vocations ministry helps the individual congregations in unexpected ways. Vocations ministry is a source of renewal and an invitation to creative ministry, in particular to creative attitudes to evangelisation of the young here in Britain. In this spirit, some congregations have undertaken vocations initiatives focused not upon promoting their own order but rather on reaching out to offer support in faith to anybody wishing to discern a vocation. Two examples are the Augustinian discernment house in Hammersmith, London, and Samuel groups supported by the Jesuits and other religious congregations.

These recent initiatives are making up for lost ground as regards vocations ministry among those in older traditions of religious life. The new movements are offering insights which we ignore at our peril and through all this, the Holy Spirit is speaking to the church. The traditional religious congregations are being called to evolve once again in response to what a new generation is saying. And the same applies, *mutatis mutandis*, to the diocesan clergy. If we wish to hear that new word from God, we need to place ourselves in the flow of the Spirit that is breathing through the church today. And the best place to catch this tide is in vocations ministry. For many people, this is a difficult word from God, as it seems to be flowing against the previous tide. Yet it need not be so. Compass is simply one example of how this might be done and other developments in vocations ministry are now growing. The challenge that vocations ministry presents to established forms of priesthood and religious life is to bring out the deep spirituality which such forms of life have never lost in new ways that respond to this new moment in the life of the church.

Reflection questions
1. The author describes three dimensions of the church: evangelisation, catechesis and *koinonia* as being attractive to young Catholics today. How might a vocations enquirer see these expressed within your own congregation?
2. What would be needed to create a vocations programme for your congregation along the lines described in this chapter?

6

Young People in Search of Religious Vocation

Joanna Gilbert

An important light is shed on religious life and vocation today by the aspirations and experiences of young discerners. As the Spirit calls a new generation to follow Christ in his way of poverty, chastity and obedience, their perceptions of religious life may offer a prophetic insight into the current and future shape of the church. Listening to the ideals, hopes, and fears of this new generation may prove at times challenging, even painful, but perhaps also encouraging. In this essay I have been invited to offer a sketch of what young people are seeking in religious life, and whether they are finding what they seek. For many who are already in religious life, listening to the voices of young discerners may take courage, generosity of spirit, and an openness to be challenged by what you hear. As with every attempt to listen and respond to the call of the Spirit in a new time, the journey will be marked by death and resurrection.

What I offer here is not a scientific presentation of statistics and trends, but some reflections which are the culmination of discussion and observation over a number of years working pastorally with people in their 20s and 30s, as well as my own experience as someone who is on a journey of discerning religious life. Additionally, some fifteen young people either currently discerning a vocation to religious life or in the early stages of religious formation have contributed their views and experiences which I have quoted throughout the essay. The questions they were asked were designed to encourage honesty and to emphasise ideals. There might be a temptation, where their views and perceptions are difficult to hear, to label or dismiss them as a minority. I think this would be to miss a valuable opportunity to listen to the voice of some very ordinary young people who are seeking to follow the call of Christ with fidelity.

The Initial Attraction

'It was during a pilgrimage to Lourdes. I was kneeling at the grotto one evening alone, and in front of me there was a young friar kneeling in his habit with a thick cord around his waist deep in prayer. Something about the solitariness of the figure in his simple garb immediately struck a chord with me' (Tim age 25).

'Seeing some Franciscan Friars of the Renewal at a youth festival: their bold appearance in habits and sandals! I was struck with a sense of the radical freedom of it, a life so different from contemporary culture, that communicated the joy of following Christ in poverty and mission' (Teresa age 29).

'Living for a year with a community of sisters who run the retreat centre where I was volunteering [...] them at the end of the day gathered together sharing stories of mission, their lives, simply delighting in each other and sharing a meal, and above all an awareness of Christ as the reason for it all' (Laura age 26).

Religious life in every age has to offer something different from the dominant culture. The initial attraction is often marked by a sense of dissatisfaction at the deepest level with the fulfilment offered by the world. The person is seeking something more, and senses it might be found by following Christ in a consecrated way.

Today we simply do not have a vast pool of potential recruits for religious to tap into. Therefore the question of what might first signal a desire to explore religious life is especially significant. The question does not dawn in the abstract; something must attract. So it is vital to ask what young people see in religious life, both positives and negatives. While the quotes above attest to life-giving encounters with religious life, this isn't the whole story. The following comments were also made, and may be uncomfortable to hear:

'I experienced a lack of vibrant, apostolic orders in the UK that seemed to fit with the charism I was seeking. Many apostolic female orders seemed to have strayed from their roots and their community life seemed secondary and poor' (Amy age 28).

'I have met religious women whose lifestyle struck me as highly secular – no different from lay people: religious sisters who seem very concerned with their appearance, or who have become 'entrepreneurs' and career-driven, or who have abandoned more traditional prayer practices for new age or Eastern experimentation' (Teresa age 29).

'Many religious no longer wear the habit, so I can't actually tell they're religious' (Jenny, age 22),

It is likely more young people would experience an initial attraction to religious life, and find ways to pursue it, if religious were more visible, placed greater emphasis on the call to evangelical witness, and were more available to young people who may want to make an initial 'disclosure' about their sense of vocation.

KEY FEATURES OF RELIGIOUS LIFE
A number of key features of religious life recur as especially significant to young people discerning and entering religious life today.

Community
Many people experience a highly fragmented society today with the breakdown of traditional forms of community. Christianity – and especially religious life – has something crucial to offer here. There is an urgent need for Christian *koinonia*: the embodiment in a people of Christ's gospel and his continued, tangible presence on earth. This Christian *koinonia* is a powerful source of evangelisation, both through witness and the welcoming of others into an experience of relationship with Christ in his church. Discerners express a desire for a shared life which includes shared vision and aspirations, a shared experience of prayer, a common mission. A sense of belonging is important to the young. The more individualised spiritual tradition of Ignatius, with its emphasis on mobility for the sake of mission, which has offered the foundation of so many religious institutions since the sixteenth century, may not hold so strong an appeal with the new generation of enquirers.

Humans are called to communion and relationship. If it is not available in religious life, they are likely to preference family life and/or wish to retain their existing network of relationships instead of joining a community. Given, especially for women, the wider opportunities available to them in life today to marry, raise a family, have a stimulating career and be an active member of a parish, aspirants would need to feel that the forms of consecrated life available offer something 'more'.

The following aspects of community are particularly worth highlighting:

Witness: is crucial both by individual religious and communities. Young people are attracted by religious in whom they perceive a joy in their chosen way of life and a unique reflection of the character of Christ. They will look for signs of fruitfulness and vitality. Amy comments: 'The presence of the Franciscan Friars and Sisters of the Renewal in the north of England and their active presence in youth ministry have actually 'proved' to many young people that religious brothers and sisters still exist. Their witness of life cannot be underestimated.'

Friendship: People have high expectations around the need and desire for intimacy. They are seeking communities that have a deep sharing of life, a strong sense of family and shared identity, and a sense of mutual support. The level of expectation may be too high, but it highlights a culture gap: the culture of 'twenty somethings' today is very focused on relationship, and the absence of visible friendship within a community appears dry and lifeless. One discerner expressed the fear of 'not having a close friend in the community I may end up living in and feeling isolated' (Rachel, age 23). A spirit of generativity is important. An institutional life must not lack a more personal dimension. Subsequently, religious living alone is likely to be off-putting to most enquirers.

Visibility and Clarity of Identity: Koinonia must take on visible forms to signal the in-breaking of the kingdom here and now; religious life is called to give particularly bold witness to the eschatological dimension of Christian life. Habits, beautiful liturgy, and other symbols communicate the values of the evangelical life. They point towards the core realities of religious life that can otherwise go unseen, making the invisible, interior dimension of the life – union with God – visible. Such symbols transcend the limitations of the person's own witness. In a highly visually articulate age, people seek beauty and symbols. Helen (age 24) says she was attracted to explore the Carmelites due to 'their beauty and simplicity'. Communities need to be able to live out and articulate their vision and charism with clarity.

Shared Vision and Aspirations: Young discerners speak of seeking a community in which they feel Christ is clearly and uncompromisingly at the centre of everything, with every element of the life flowing out of this relationship. They also seek communities characterised by high aspirations, zeal and fervour: 'I am seeking a community that has high aspirations, that has its eyes focused on doing the will of God and loving God' (Ben, age 25). As Judith Eydmann at the National Office for Vocation observes: 'Articulating and defining the charism on paper is not sufficient, it has to be visible in the way in which it is lived out by the community.' A real sense of integrity is vital. Many aspirants seek communities rooted in a deep and solid tradition, who are living with fidelity to their founding charism: 'My aspiration is to be part of the history of the church through an established order' (Rachel). A tradition is particularly appealing if it has a sense of distinctiveness and clear identity, which can be well articulated by the members.

Structure and Discipline: The 'monastic form' seems to be generally attracting larger numbers of enquirers. This is evidenced by the style of the new, growing communities like the Community of St John, the Jerusalem Community, and the healthy novitiate of apostolic orders like the Dominican Friars in England. Common to all these communities are the habit, public liturgy / common prayer, times and places of silence, a structured day, and ordered community life.

Liminality: The major renewal movements of the church have been characterised by poverty and renunciation, moving towards the margins of church and society in order to again live an uncompromising discipleship of Christ. Such withdrawal from a Christianity adapted to secular needs, enables a greater evangelistic witness and mission. People today seek a life that is different from secular living, with a marked contrast of values and way of life, highlighting the prophetic dimension to a life consecrated to Christ. Amy observes that 'many of the contemplative orders in the UK are still attractive to young people, because of their counter-cultural life'. The truly evangelical life is attractive: 'Young people are attracted to radical living.' Not modelled on domestic forms of living, but distinctively Christian and clearly centred on encounter with Christ, a structured community life can enable its members to live out the gospel in sharp contrast to the dominant culture around them. One young religious in formation commented that 'Orthodox Catholicism is extraordinarily radical if we take the teachings of the church seriously; traditional religious life is profoundly countercultural if lived properly. Too many congregations see radicalism as rebelling against the religious life of the 1950s, and in the process they have come to look very secular and normal: they can end up saying exactly the same things as the general culture' (Br Matthew, age 25). Many enquirers seek a certain rigour of life: 'I am put off by seeing the vow of poverty not being lived literally – some communities I've visited seem to have more possessions, spend more money and generally live a more luxurious life than I currently do' (Jenny, age 22).

Fidelity to the church: Engaged young Catholic adults are 'looking for communities who love the Lord, therefore love the church that he founded and all her teachings […] and whose entire existence is about falling more in love with them both and encouraging others to do the same' (Amy). Having grown up in a morally permissive society, where secularisation threatens previously accepted Christian values, young Catholics want to know what the church teaches. There can be a perception among the young that the previous generation lost a strong sense of rooting in the wisdom of the Christian tradition, at times even abandoning it for new ideologies. For many young people, this comes from (sometimes painful) personal experience of growing up in Catholic families, parishes and schools without receiving convincing teaching about the faith, leaving them struggling in an aggressively secular world. The post-Vatican II generation was perhaps able to be complacent about Christian teaching because they had received a thorough, though perhaps overly rigid, faith formation. Young people today often do not feel they have grasped the basics. They look to role models/teachers of the faith for courage in holding to and proclaiming moral teachings that may be unpopular or even unfathomable in a very liberal society. 'Young people are attracted to teaching that is not watered down, even if it is difficult' (Amy).

Prayer and Spirituality: Principally, enquirers seek a way of life that is rooted in relationship with Christ above all else: 'Essential to me in religious life is a community that keeps God as the absolute centre of everything' (John, age 26). They look for a level of structure that can safeguard times and spaces for prayer, ensuring this ultimate focus cannot be threatened by any other pressures or demands: a way of life which integrates personal and common prayer into the rhythm of the day. Daily Mass is cited as the vital source of communion with God/others, giving shape and meaning to all mission. Miriam (age 26) says: 'Some of the key features I seek in religious life are daily Mass and adoration, and frequent opportunities for the sacrament of reconciliation.' Eucharistic adoration has become a significant feature of the new communities and movements. Again, given the wider life opportunities available today especially for women, aspirants would need to feel that the forms of consecrated life available offer something 'more', and the prayer dimension here is key. If an aspirant perceives they can have just as much time for prayer with a family and/or job, why enter religious life? Many religious appear too busy; Mike (age 23) said: 'I looked at an apostolic-contemplative order and found that the lack of time available for private prayer was fairly off-putting.'

For religious formed before Vatican II into strong routines of personal prayer through a structured/disciplined life of common prayer, this has perhaps enabled them to sustain the practice of prayer in much more fragmented and autonomous expressions of apostolic religious life after the council. A young person entering cannot be assumed to have much formation or discipline in prayer and will need the structure of common prayer to form them.

MISSION / EVANGELISATION

A few particular aspects can be highlighted:

Witness: Religious life, faithful to the evangelical counsels as the means to a deeper conformity to Christ, should send out the bold message of faith, hope and love. Our world needs this above all, and the call is urgent. Providing for material needs and human rights is incredibly valuable work, but ultimately the call of the church is to signal a hope that can sustain us through all the suffering of this present life: a greater reality that can give meaning and shape even to pain and sorrow. This is the vision of the beatitudes. An essential aspect of this witness is community (communion or *koinonia*). Our current cultural context calls for the incarnation of Christ within a community that witnesses to the joy and fruitfulness of gospel living.

Rooted in Christ: All fruitful mission flows out of communion with Christ. The contemplative dimension needs to underpin and penetrate through a whole apostolate, bringing a strong eschatological dimension to all apostolic work. People seek from religious something far more than secular skills or social work; they seek a certain 'quality of presence' that is born significantly out of deep encounter with Christ in the silence of personal prayer, sacred reading, and study. Their work must be noticeably different from humanism or activism.

A common mission: A shared apostolate or, at least, a clear sense of common mission potentially builds communion, fraternal relationships, and purpose: 'To be companions like the apostles on a mission' (Rachel). It also gives greater visibility, and witnesses to a common life: 'Of real importance for me is a shared experience and shared mission (not ten people living together with ten completely different missions)' (Laura). A mission that is given its unique character through the fruitfulness of deep rooting within a tradition/fidelity to a charism creates a sense of coherence and shared identity.

Proclaiming the gospel: It is attractive for young people to encounter religious who speak boldly and articulately about the gospel, their own faith and vocation, and are confident teachers of Catholic belief. This means being rooted in scripture and tradition, and engaged in life-long distinctively Christian formation of oneself. Many Catholics today appear to have lost faith in proclaiming Christ and the teachings of the church. When young people see this in role models like religious, their own faith can be undermined.

Distinctively Catholic: Many will seek a distinctively Catholic-Christian, prophetic mission, something they feel they cannot do as easily as lay people (especially given many other forms of service are now accessible to the laity, e.g. teaching, nursing, social work) i.e. a work born out of the other core aspects of their life – prayer, study, community. In an increasingly secular society, they may wish to find ways to serve as Christians and spread the gospel message that are not hindered or compromised by secular pressures or restrictions. Work that is connected to their own community and not tied to the ethos/charism of another institution tends to be preferable. And in a time when church ministry can feel depleted and under-resourced, especially facing the attacks of growing secularism, enquirers may look for communities that give a strong importance to study and contemplation as vital sources for mission, and who are engaged in the urgent work of offering in-depth Christian formation.

Reaching the Margins: Enquirers may aspire to an apostolate that reaches people on the margins of church and society, without being assimilated into secular life, seeking ways to reach out beyond traditional institutions. Communities which appear to be simply maintaining themselves are less attractive than those with a strong gospel mission responding to the needs of the world.

New Forms of Consecrated Life

'One of the gifts of the Spirit to our time is undoubtedly the flourishing of the ecclesial movements' (Pope John Paul II).

'Apostolic movements appear in ever new forms in history – necessarily so, because they are the Holy Spirit's answer to the ever changing situations in which the church lives' (Pope Benedict XVI).

Across Europe and the US we have seen the development of many new ecclesial movements and new forms of religious life since Vatican II. Pope Benedict, as Cardinal Ratzinger, spoke in 1998 of the phenomenon of the new movements within the wider historical perspective, pointing out how at certain periods of the church's history there have been widespread movements of the Spirit renewing the church: 'Movements generally derive their origin from a charismatic leader and take shape in concrete communities, inspired by the life of their founder; they attempt to live the gospel anew, in its totality, and recognise the church without hesitation as the ground of their life without which they could not exist.' Examples include the monastic movement of the third and fourth centuries, the Franciscan movement of the thirteenth century and the Jesuits in the sixteenth century.

A number of young people from the UK consider trying their

vocation with new communities and movements abroad. However, increasingly these communities are developing foundations here: the Franciscan Friars and Sisters of the Renewal now have a number of houses in the UK and Ireland, and the Brothers of the St John Community are also now established here. Other communities are likely to come, and perhaps some home-grown will emerge too. The ecclesial movements, however, are still struggling to take root, but certainly the Catholic Charismatic Renewal, Youth 2000 and the community to which I belong, the Wellspring Community, demonstrate a trend slowly emerging here also, which is impacting on the vocational interest of young people and the shape of religious life.

A striking feature of the new ecclesial movements is the renewed sense of the church as one organic communion: one Body of Christ in which all the parts, gifted by the one Spirit, play a significant role. The new movements properly understood are not 'lay communities': they are often characterised by the sharing of one charism or vision by laity (married and single of all ages), clergy and bishops, and male and female consecrated members. In some cases the uniting charism is a rooting in a major spiritual tradition of the church. In many cases, consecrated men and women live alongside one another (though with separate accommodation) sharing some aspects of their living, e.g. liturgy, apostolate. The shared charism enables fruitful collaboration with the laity, often through support of lay formation and mission work together, but with clear boundaries respecting the difference of vocations.

The new movements are creating a renewed 'seed-bed for vocations'. By an emphasis on the universal call to holiness of all the baptised, and the witness they offer to a vibrant, Spirit-filled life of faith, often not experienced in parishes, they are bringing the proposal of Christ before young people in an urgent and attractive way. While drawing vocations to their own forms of life, lay and religious, their impact has also been to inspire and nurture vocations to traditional orders and diocesan priesthood as well. The impact of groups like Youth 2000 and the charismatic renewal are evidence of this in our own country. These movements are in touch with young Christians, and, where authentic, are dedicated not to 'recruitment' but to mission and the formation of young Christians, giving a future to the church. Their success highlights the 'gap' that exists and needs to be bridged between many existing and well-established religious communities, and where young people are today. This is especially a problem for women's apostolic congregations. Increasingly, male apostolic orders such as the English Benedictines, Dominicans and Carmelites are working collaboratively with new movements in the evangelisation and formation of young people.

HIGHLIGHTING SOME CHALLENGES AND FEARS

Inevitably young aspirants' experiences and perceptions of religious life are not always positive. Some themes seem to be recurrent when asked what they might have found off-putting about religious life.

Vitality and Zeal: The most dominant appears to be principally about witness to a life-giving way. Young people are turned off by a lack of vitality and zeal found in some communities and their members. It is not uncommon to hear a young enquirer say they encountered apathy or a lack of hope and vision. The following comments were made in response to the question: 'What puts you off religious life?':

> 'A lack of interior happiness, optimism and enthusiasm – not in terms of mood which changes for us all when we go through troubles, but a deeper thing that is there even in difficulties: this is probably the number one off-putting thing' (John).
> 'I experienced a lack of vibrant, apostolic orders in the UK' (Amy).
> 'Complacency, timidity, small horizons' (Ben).

Common life: Overly domestic styles of living give the impression of a community settled in its comfort zones: 'In some communities the style of life seems centred around TV and card games: just too comfortable, and like married life but without the benefits' (Teresa, age 29). Religious life can be perceived as marked by a high level of individualism and autonomy. For some communities, community life has simply never been a strong part of their charism. For others, there has been an abandonment of many practices and customs that built communion, for instance common prayer, common table, and common times of silence.

Age and generation gap: Another important fear is of joining an aging or dying congregation. For many, the age gaps appear simply too wide to be bridged. Many feel it would be unnatural and unhealthy to join a community in their 20s when the next youngest members are in their 50s, 60s or older.

'I'm afraid of joining a community which has no-one/few people of my generation or even the generation above me, where I could possibly be the last to join; I fear the lack of peer companionship and understanding of the church/spirituality in which I have grown up. I am put off by communities which seem to be slowly dying: less numbers, and a reduced mission, or mission which is no longer distinct from social work (i.e. mission without distinct sense of community or spirituality) – what journey would I be joining?' (Laura).

'I fear joining an aging order with no or few people of my own age, and no-one to share the journey of formation with. It would be really hard to have a mission together if most members are retired, and the younger members may be needed either for nursing care or to earn money to support the community' (Teresa).

'A lot of communities in the UK only have elderly members, which worries me because if I joined, they would die in a few years and I'd be left all by myself without a community' (Jenny).

Communities with young people inevitably attract more young people. There are, as in every era, differences of agenda between the generations, noticeably in areas like liturgy, teaching on moral theology, and the form mission work should take eg the post-Vatican II generation's peace and justice agenda *vs* the John Paul II's 'new evangelisation'.

'Several orders seemed to be underpinned by secular feminism, rather than the Catholic understanding of femininity and the dignity of women in this light, as taught by John Paul II' (Amy).

'I once spoke with a monk who seemed to be from a totally different generation and did not seem to have a solid grasp on the world and pressures that young people face today' (Mike).

Women and religious life: Women's religious life presents specific challenges. It appears to offer little in the middle-ground between enclosed-contemplative life and apostolic life which often verges towards the style of secular institutes. Some young women would welcome the emergence of communities from some of the major spiritual traditions of the church which mirror the contemplative-apostolic balance of male communities, such as the Carmelites and Benedictines. The ministry and role of women in the church is a source of uncertainty. The priesthood gives clarity of role, and priest-religious can feel a sense that their work will always be of value, no matter what changes may occur in society. Many religious congregations, particularly of women, have seen their work alter radically in recent decades, resulting from shifts in the needs of society. This may leave young women uncertain about the stability of their mission and ministry, that it may undergo fundamental shifts. Subsequently, communities with a charism that can transcend such societal changes may appear more secure. There are challenges here for how women's roles are given a sense of authority and support by the institutional church and especially the clergy / male religious. Given that their role is less clear, visible, and potentially less valued, it therefore needs a strong sense of identity and purpose. Have many women turned to secular skills to try to achieve this status and role? Healing therapies, or business skills, or management jargon? A greater emphasis on resourcing ministry from within the Christian tradition – scripture, theology, spirituality rooted in a tradition – may strengthen identity and role.

Conclusion

Crucially, young people are seeking something 'more' from religious life. If they do not believe it offers a more perfect way of following Christ, that it will be life-giving for them and others, and that it would be impossible to live their faith as radically by remaining as they are or marrying, why would they choose religious life? Increasingly, many committed young Catholics have a strong prayer life and experience of community, and already work voluntarily or in paid roles in church ministry. What is the 'more' that religious life can offer that will make it a worthwhile choice for a discerner to pursue? Religious life must be distinctive and clear in communicating its value as a life-giving way of following Christ and responding to his gospel. Thus the perceptions and experiences of young adults today poses a significant, but also exciting, challenge for the church: the need for an ever deeper renewal, in particular of the witness religious life gives to Christ, the distinctive form this life must take, and of the kind of work we must all do to foster a culture of vocation.

Reflection questions

1. What is your reaction to the critique of religious life offered by the young adults quoted in this essay? How would you respond to their comments if you were in conversation with them?

2. How does your congregation fit within the headings outlined above of crucial factors sought by vocations enquirers today?

7

The Dominicans and Vocations

Gerard Dunne OP

Introduction

I would like to preface the remarks that follow by noting that this contribution deals with the vocations situation in Ireland for the Dominicans in the past ten year period. I am aware that since this is to be considered in an English context that the English Dominicans have had some considerable success in that time-frame also. However, the method of vocational promotion and discernment are quite different in both provinces – as well as the social, religious and cultural context. That said, it is reasonable to say that the Dominicans of the English and Irish provinces have been widely regarded as having a significant increase both in interest in the order and actual vocations to their provinces.

Context

The Irish Dominicans at their Provincial Chapter in 2000 recognised the seriousness of their situation regarding both vocations and formation. That year there was just one man in formation – in a province of approximately 200 friars. The numbers joining the province had almost ceased, allied with the fact that a significant number of men in formation had left the order during the 1990s. It is reasonable to say that both formation and vocations were no longer a high priority for the province. There were some tangible reasons for this. Firstly, the work of vocations director/promoter had been one of a number of ministries assigned to one particular friar in the province. It was evident that this could not continue. Secondly, there were two houses of formation in the province – one for the novitiate, the other for the studentate (those who enter into formation after the novitiate) which had done sterling work in forming our brothers for many years but who had become somewhat tired and stale in continuing this task. Thirdly, Ireland had changed dramatically and it was clear that the 'old way' of doing formation was no longer working nor indeed was the way in which the culture of vocations was promoted. There was a need for a radical re-think and overhaul for these vital works. Fourthly, it was clear that while there was still interest in the order it was from a somewhat older generation than heretofore. How to accommodate these people needed to be addressed. Fifthly, the question of communicating the work and ministry of the Dominicans in Ireland was not very good. The chapter set about making some changes in how to better communicate ourselves. Sixthly, admissions procedures were highly outdated and not serving the needs of a new century and not in keeping with all the various guidelines laid down by the church and the ongoing child protection procedures in place. The chapter appointed an admissions board to overhaul the various structures of admission.

Actions of the Provincial Chapter

Taking the above situation into account, the brethren at the Provincial Chapter in 2000 decided to (1) appoint a full-time vocations director for the province. This friar would have no other responsibilities other than this ministry and would be resourced as much as was necessary. This was a bold, but vital move. It would not have been easy for the province to release a man full-time into this ministry considering the various needs of the province as a whole. (2) The novitiate and studentate were moved from the locations in which they were situated to new locations. This was a dramatic moment because it had many implications for the communities who were heretofore communities of formation and, as one might expect, it placed a new burden on the two new chosen communities. It was a difficult and painful move – one that sent shockwaves around the province because it meant the wholesale re-assignment of many of the friars to facilitate this necessary change. However, it did send a strong signal that the province was serious about the question of formation and vocations. (3) New formation personnel were appointed and the new formation communities were supplemented in order to facilitate the smooth changeover to being communities of formation. Our constant objective was to make the experience of formation a positive one for those who were about to join us. (4) In trying to integrate potential candidates who were slightly older (i.e. 28-35 years) to the province, many from highly qualified academic and work backgrounds, plans were set in place at the level of formation and studies to best accommodate these new interested candidates. It was clear that the 'one-size-fits-all' attitude that we had to formation was no longer workable. (5) Up to the year 2000 the Irish Dominicans had not had any credible or real presence on the internet or in the media in general. Because of this lack, the Provincial Chapter put in place a team of friars to highlight the work and ministry of the Dominicans in Ireland – again with all the necessary resources, financial and otherwise, in place. (6) The Admissions Board, with the consent of the province introduced new and more stringent procedures of admission for interested candidates. These procedures included the engagement of psychological and psychiatric testing by qualified consultants. This had previously been carried out by religious, and had proved unsatisfactory.

It must be pointed out here that the following two Provincial Chapters of the Irish Province has continued to endorse these radical decisions made in the year 2000 and are constantly monitored and reviewed at provincial level to gauge their effectiveness.

Outcome of the Acts of the Provincial Chapter 2000
The outcome of these decisions taken by the Provincial Chapter and subsequent chapters are as follows:

(1) The appointment of a full time vocations director (one friar has held this position for the past ten years – myself) has seen enquiries about the order grow steadily from approximately fifteen per year in 2000, to an average of sixty in the past two to three years. This has been a gradual and steady increase. Since 2000, thirty-two men have been admitted to the province, four of these are now ordained, twenty-three are currently in formation at various levels and five have left the order at various stages. It is interesting to draw a comparative note here: in the 1990s the rate of attrition (drop-out) was over fifty per cent; in the past ten years, that rate has fallen well below ten per cent. Collaboration with the other entities of the order, namely the contemplative nuns, the apostolic sisters and the lay

Dominicans has been a crucial part of the work of the vocations director – this collaboration has significantly raised the Dominican profile in Ireland to such an extent that there is an annual vocations seminar for all the branches of the Dominican family at various times during the year – drawing large numbers. The appointment of a full time director has allowed much greater scope in promoting the friars – particularly in third level institutes and colleges and also has allowed for a far more serious discernment process to be undertaken with serious candidates. Any such serious discernment process for us lasts at the very minimum one year and, more regularly, two years. However, the most important outcome of the appointment of a full time vocations director has been the giving of time to enquirers and candidates. We take every enquiry, person and candidate very seriously because we realise that in the vocational field, they are the most important constituent element. This has allowed the role of vocations director to become very pastoral in nature – and the feedback is that this is highly valued by candidates.

(2) The move of both novitiate and studentate was highly significant in that it allowed a new impetus towards formation to emerge. The province decided to set up these formation communities where the primary concern would be formation. This also allowed other ministries to flourish at the same time – a particularly valuable witness for those taking the first steps in Dominican life. Also, the province decided to assign brethren to the houses of formation who were mainly young (under forty years) to somehow bridge the gap in age between the older generations and the young. In the main, this has worked very well and it can safely be said that, despite some teething difficulties in the early years of these new projects, the primary focus on formation has paid dividends. It should also be noted that the generational divide was not as problematic as we envisaged when starting off – in fact the witness of our older members has a deep impact on the ongoing vocations of our brothers in formation. In taking formation seriously, the communities use all the vehicles constitutionally at their disposal, to discuss and reflect on the formation project. Communication here is absolutely key, i.e. between the formation communities and those in formation themselves.

(3) It should also be noted that the province has made many sacrifices for formation, particularly in the area of personnel in that some of our friars in charge of formation were taken out of very important ministries to support the work of formation. Again, for our novices and students this shows that we are taking both our formation and theirs very seriously indeed. Insofar as it has been possible, all our formatters have undergone training and are constantly evaluating the needs of the formation system. In any such situation as this, it is crucial to have the support and backing of the Provincial Council or leadership team. I know that on every agenda of our Provincial Council which meets twelve to fifteen times a year are two constant items: vocations and formation. It shows the seriousness and level of commitment at leadership level.

(4) Crucial to the work of formation in the Irish Dominican context has been the level of communication with each individual on how best to shape his academic, spiritual, human and Dominican formation. From the very beginning, a young friar is consulted on these various aspects of formation – along, of course, with others interested in their welfare at these levels. Our feedback has shown that the younger friars deeply appreciate the level of commitment and enthusiasm shown towards their formation. In so far as it is possible, the province tries to keep the younger brothers in formation together for the initial years before they are sent to various academic centres in Ireland and abroad for studies. This is to give them a real sense of the life of the province to which they want to belong. As an aside, the Irish Dominicans hope, in the next two to three years to re-establish a faculty of theology in Ireland. This would help greatly in forming our younger friars together in a Dominican context. While Dominicans often quote the fact that 'one is responsible for one's own formation', it has to be said that the province has not spared in giving proper resources and funding to allow this to happen.

(5) Communications: Over ninety per cent of enquiries to the vocations director come through the internet and electronic media. It goes without saying that a presence on the internet is, and will continue to be crucial. The province has a good website. Many of the friars have set up web logs, and are conversant with

the various social media outlets. The province, too, has increased its exposure through all the various Catholic media services in Ireland to the point that the profile of the Order has never been higher. Indeed, the province actively supports the initiatives of the brethren in this area as a means of communicating more effectively our work and mission. This is an ongoing and ever-changing medium and we are constantly trying to find new ways of letting others know of our Dominican identity.

(6) Concerning admissions to the Order: The province has overhauled its admission process. Candidates are accompanied for a defined period as laid down by the vocations director which constitutes their postulancy. They are exposed to communities from an early stage in that process. They are given all necessary information by way of books and other relevant reading material. They meet regularly with other friars who are involved in other disciplines. The process of admission takes several weeks from comprehensive applications, to supplying of references, to police clearance, to exhaustive interviews with the provincial admissions board and the professional assistance of medical and psychological experts. The board charged with advising the provincial as to whether to accept candidates or not normally spend a week living with the candidates as part of the admissions process. While it is exhaustive, we have found that the candidates value enormously that their applications are taken so seriously. The admissions process is constantly evaluated, year on year and the admissions board meets regularly each year to plan the process of admission.

The above list is of course not at all exhaustive, but they are the most important steps that the Irish Dominicans have taken in the past number of years in relation to vocations and formation.

Candidates – and what attracts them

It would be important to refer to the types of candidates that are attracted to the Irish Dominicans and to say a word on what it is that attracts them. The average profile of our candidates is mid 20s to mid 30s. Generally, they are educated to third level and the vast majority have at least a primary degree. A large number would have a secondary degree while a percentage would have doctorates. A number would be working professionally and the minority would have a secondary education and/or working in unskilled jobs.

When asked what attracts candidates to the Irish Dominicans, I normally respond by saying that there are three reasons: (1) An authentic community life. By that I mean a regular and observant attitude to religious life, common prayer, a serious concern for study and a strong preaching identity. As religious in Ireland, the Dominicans regularly wear their religious habit. It is not unnoticed by enquirers. (2) The tradition of the order. By that I mean that they see in us a willingness to take what is good out of the tradition of the order to a contemporary generation. The fact that the Irish Dominicans have initiated new projects, particularly in the academic and pastoral fields in recent years has animated many to become involved in our way of life and (3) the deepening of the relationship with God in a communal context. This really ought to be the main attraction to the order and I think the new generation see something in us that we do not see in ourselves: namely this ongoing Dominican inquisitive quest to know the Lord more deeply through our prayer, common life and study. At least these are the reasons that the candidates offer as to why they wish to join us. Of course, the lives of the brethren themselves are more often than not a real and tangible reason for attracting others.

Conclusion

You will see from this brief account that the Irish Dominicans have had courage to make changes – primarily because they were forced to. We are certainly not a perfect province. We have the same difficulties as other congregations of religious, both male and female. We are, however, committed to the future of the province. The province has not been afraid to invest in its future and while this has been painful for some, the dividends are clear to see. The Irish Dominicans believe passionately in the charism of the order, but believe passionately too in handing on that charism to a new generation. A new generation has responded to this. We hope that the Lord will continue to call others to this project.

Reflection questions

1. What problems in their approach to vocations ministry did the Irish Dominicans detect? How do these compare with your own vocations strategy?

2. What changes did they make? What difference do you think these made? What changes might you make to your own vocations strategy in the light of this essay?

PART THREE

Forward into the Future

8

Religious Life: A Question of Visibility

Gemma Simmonds CJ

During my background research for the launch of a new course in the theology of religious life for the Religious Life Institute at Heythrop College in London, I came across an unlikely resource in a film clip on YouTube from the Oprah Winfrey show. In it her researcher, Lisa Ling, spends a day and a night in the convent of the recently-founded Dominican Sisters of Mary, Mother of the Eucharist. What one sees in this film is a highly visible form of religious life for women, the like of which most seasoned religious have not seen since their own novitiate, or perhaps never at all. Large numbers of fresh-faced young women in their teens and early twenties are living a strongly-regulated form of religious life, with every signal in terms of habit, community lifestyle, apostolate and prayer in common that this is a life wholly 'other'. My own early experience of something like this in the mid-1970s was the last gasp in Britain of religious life as it had been lived before Vatican II, a life, for me, soon to enter into a lengthy process of deconstruction. The only time I have witnessed it since was in the 1990s in Romania, in the immediate aftermath of the downfall of communism, when religious life was restored along the model of what communism had destroyed some four decades previously.

I showed the film clip to a class of twenty four students, mostly female religious, though two were laymen. Reactions were predictably varied. They ranged from relief not to be living this model of religious life anymore, disbelief that it was re-emerging after so much effort to break away from it to honest jealousy at the sight of a community with so many young people in it. I showed the film during a class exploring the topic of visibility. I chose to end the course with this because I have found, in my talks around the world on religious life, that there is no other topic guaranteed to raise the room temperature quite so fast.

What is it about religious life being visible that poses such a challenge? For many religious the obvious visual signals once available about the 'different' nature of religious life offered a certain security. As soon as you entered an order or congregation everything from the clothes to the furniture and the way you were now expected to move or speak or eat proclaimed that you had embarked upon a life significantly different from what you had known. To some the clear boundaries and strong sense of identity afforded by gradual inculturation into religious life offered reassurance and confidence, whether it was learning to keep one's eyes downcast 'a coffin's length' or, in the case of the old rule of my own congregation, to 'season their conversation with pious reflections to the edification of those that hear them'. To others it represented the gradual erosion or thwarted development of a sense of adult, integrated self and the imposition of a barrage of customs as bizarre as they were unnecessary in pursuit of the following of the Christ who calls each of us to have life and have it to the full.

If the lifestyle of religious prior to the council aimed at showing that it was of another order entirely from life in the *saeculum*, the most obvious outcome of *aggiornamento* has been to render much of religious life effectively invisible, both internally to those living it and externally to those who witness it. The stress given by the council to the universal call to holiness, the call to return *ad fontes* and to re-identify ourselves with our founding charism led precisely to a repudiation of the sort of visibility that many experienced as inauthentic to the nature and purpose of religious consecration. Many religious congregations of women and some of the brothers' orders developed in a similar way to the Béghard and Béguine communities, who had no aspirations to canonical structures. They had those structures imposed on them from without by a church anxious to control the impulses of its more charismatic groups and members. The call to return *ad fontes* thus proved problematic when they found that they had been subsumed into an identity, construct and lifestyle at odds with the spiritual impulse of their origins. 'Tradition', for such groups, came to mean something quite other than what they had lived within recent memory, so that a return to tradition came to look like deconstruction, but was in fact a reclaiming of an original, charismatic identity.

Recent events within the church have shown that a highly visible and differentiated lifestyle were, alas, no guarantee of holiness or integrity in living the vows we professed. There is evidence to suggest that indeed in some cases it provided (perhaps unconsciously) a helpful screen behind which to hide a multiplicity of social, psychological and sexual pathologies. It would be well for the young vocations enquirers who are quoted in other chapters of this book, critical as they are of 'invisible' religious life, to consider this. But if our move away from a visibility many found exclusive and triumphalist was a sign of a healthy humility and an obedience to Vatican II's emphasis on the primacy of the baptismal vocation and the universal call to holiness, it must be admitted that this process of disappearing into the woodwork has also posed some significant problems. A new generation of vocational searchers is challenging the meaning of what we have done, though significantly there are also a good many searchers, especially women over the age of thirty, who feel drawn to religious life precisely because it has liberated itself from external trappings they perceive as stifling and meaningless.

To some commentators it was the loss of this differentiation that sounded the death-knell of apostolic religious life, at least for women. If we lived to all extents and purposes like everyone else, except with fewer creature comforts and the inconvenience of companions we had not chosen, in what sense was that consecration? For others, who through deconstruction became more inserted into the lives of the people they served, it represented a much-needed and healthy liberation from the false trappings of holiness which separated us from adult autonomy, integrated humanity and apostolic effectiveness. Yet the last two Popes have been persistent in their calls to religious to return to a more visible and distinctive way of life. These calls appear to be echoed by a number of young people in search of religious life who are attracted to what is strongly distinct and identifiable as something other than the secular lifestyle and values they wish to leave behind. Where we have been keen to show how the best of gospel values are compatible with the best aspirations of decent-minded human beings, they are keen to preach the uniqueness and particularity of a gospel with which they do not feel themselves to have been effectively evangelised by their parents' generation. Religious have been agonising about a crisis of vocations since shortly after the council. My own experience as a vocations director is that there is not, in fact, that critical a shortage of vocations. I am regularly contacted by women (and some men) seeking help in discerning a call to radical service of God. What I do perceive is that we are dealing not so much with a crisis of vocations as a massive crisis of culture, and we have barely begun to address it.

What are we to make of critiques like those found elsewhere in this book? Is the call to distinctiveness merely another chapter in the inexorable process of revisionism and restorationism that many see as currently engulfing the church? Is the question of visibility just another increasingly desperate ploy in strategies of recruitment? Is the desire to be distinctive an expression of spiritual narcissism, psycho-social immaturity and world-denying ecclesiology, or is there a wisdom within this desire that we would be foolish to ignore? Could it possibly be that, despite the undoubtedly faithful and generous efforts at renewal over the past fifty years, we simply got this one wrong, or we got it right for its time, but now a new time and new context have overtaken us?

Because the question of visibility so often gets immediately linked to whether or not we should look different, I am going to stress here that what I am talking about is distinctiveness or particularity rather than just external cultural signals. I think there are two aspects to visibility – one is intra-visibility, the way in which we signify to ourselves what is distinctive about our life, and one is extra-visibility, the way in which we convey that distinctiveness to others. I am indebted for these reflections to the members of my Theology of Religious Life course.

It seems reasonable that we should want the life we have chosen, or rather the life which has chosen us, to have a clear identity. I remember speaking some years ago to a novice in her thirties who had made considerable sacrifices to enter religious life in search of 'something more' than her previous life as a devout, single, committed Catholic. She had been moved to a community where, she said, the house was awash with aromatherapy oil, but she was yet to experience a single prayer prayed together in community. The only constant within the house timetable was the soap opera *Coronation Street*. For her this was neither religious nor life – she saw more coherence in the way she had been living before. She still had a sense that what she desired was to be found in the consecrated life, but in her current context any sense of meaning and distinctiveness attached to that life had effectively been rendered invisible by those living it as an empty shell.

I suspect that the problem is in part an ecclesiological one. Part of the historical development of religious life has been that its emergence was not only a flight from the power structures and values of the world, but also an alternative path within a church whose own power structures were seen to reflect those of the world too closely into a more radical and liminal form of life. Religious life has at its heart vows that opt in the most radical way against the fundamental human drives towards mastery and possession through power, sex and money. Although particular religious or religious orders have not been immune from corruption within their history that sense of being part of an alternative even to what is happening within the church has been a perennial pattern and it has not been without conflict. One has only to look at the early reception by the church of the vocations of a Francis of Assisi, a Mary Ward or a Mary McKillop to understand. This has long caused tensions between the hierarchy and religious, and it is interesting to note that one of the bishops reported as leading the move at the Second Vatican Council to have all religious brought under the control of the bishops was none other than Karol Wotyla, later Pope John Paul II. His own relations with religious were not always of the most appreciative and part of his critique of the abandonment by religious of their distinctive features was due to his sense that by giving them up they were assimilating themselves to a secular, consumer-driven culture that had little bearing on the gospel. He also seems to have seen it as going hand in hand with a do-it-yourself, go-your-own-way individualism deriving from either the capitalist or Marxist ideologies of which he was one of the twentieth century's greatest critics.[1]

1. Gemma Simmonds, 'John Paul II and the Consecrated Life' in *The Vision of John Paul II: Assessing his Thought and Influence*, Gerard Mannion ed., (Collegeville, Liturgical Press, 2008) pp 200-214.

It is common among religious to hear stringent critiques of 'the church', as if the church was a 'them' set in conflict against an 'us'. Religious life attracts many radicals, and radicals do not always sit happily within authoritarian systems. Among women religious there is a torrent of evidence across the world of being bullied by priests and bishops (and not a few male religious). Among religious brothers there are centuries of experience of being belittled or ignored by those rejoicing in the power of priesthood. Among missionaries there is a relentless catalogue of struggling on behalf of the poor, sometimes at cost of their very lives, in the face of a church that has made alliances with the wealthy and powerful that it is anxious to defend. All this can lead to a disillusionment and cynicism about the church as a 'them' by religious who take refuge in their sense that their consecration leads to a more bearable, more liberated and gospel authentic 'us'. But this is a false dichotomy which can easily lead to its own idolatries and to a disengagement with the very source and context of their vows.

Religious life is mandated by the church. The vows that we make are public, and there is a mutuality within the way they are lived in the wider community of the church and the world, as there is in the vows of marriage. While the life of the vows is something each person works out within their own skin, as it were, our gradual entry into the dynamic of poverty, chastity and obedience, or whatever other vows we take, marks us out as incarnating specific virtues for the sake of the Body of Christ that is humanity. We become people for others, incarnating in ways seen and unseen the mystery of God's indwelling in human lives. In their own turn the people of God continue to respond, whatever the disappointments and disillusionments of recent revelations, to the ideals and purpose contained within a vowed life in community expressed in self-giving (and self-fulfilling) ministry.

When religious life becomes too much of an individual construct, based mainly on what religious feel personally attracted to or moved to at a given moment, it is in danger of becoming a form of systematised narcissism. It is not for nothing that the prayer of the church is commonly known in monastic circles as 'the work of God'. It is precisely work, even at times a chore, rather than a form of self-expression or self-fulfilment. Those whose charism it is to recite the hours on a regular basis do it as part of the more general *kenosis* involved in religious life, giving of their time, energy and attention to a task that can at times feel unbearably repetitive and humdrum. This is not always helped by a breviary that makes no concessions to context, especially that of women, so that communities of women find themselves chanting meaninglessly the refrain: 'Lord Jesus, we are your brothers.' But the replacement of the word of God by an array of chiffon scarves, tea lights, indigenous poetry and whale singing is itself as culturally determined as the worst excesses of exclusive androcentric language. Furthermore while it may speak strongly to those jaded by decades of the breviary it is often even more foreign to young adults, thirsty for the word of God celebrated by the faith community, than Latin itself. Part of the mandate of religious is to pray the prayer of the church as well as to pray in a way that expresses their own deepest longings. We do this as part of our call to be transformed by prayer, vow and mission for our own sake but principally for that of the church and the world. We rightly seek that transformation in authentic relationships, solidarity with the poor and broken and vibrant experiences of the Spirit among and within us in prayer. But it is also to be found in the formal exercises of our religious profession. Discerners of religious vocation justifiably hope that they will find this willingness to be conformed to the likeness of Christ among us. When they do not, they go elsewhere.

One of the male religious in my class who saw the Oprah Winfrey film clip disliked what he saw as being too 'in your face'. This may be a question of taste, but it seems worth pointing out that there is something inherently 'in your face' about what moved the first proto-religious to leave the city and go into the desert in search of an all-or-nothing following of Christ. The subsequent history of religious life has been of a series of 'in your face' gestures in response both to an inner call and to an external imperative within society itself. Many of us will have experienced that sort of passion for extremes as adolescents or young adults, perhaps to have it tempered in later life by experience of our own frailty and that of our companions, or a sense of the fragility of all human fantasies including the fantasy of a holiness that lies in what is above or beyond the ordinary.

We live in a world which communicates strongly and instantly via sophisticated visual media, and we cannot expect the generations of today and tomorrow to be immune from this. It is no longer the word that is made flesh for them so much as the image, and so it is natural that they should hope that religious will provide a clear and compelling image of 'the hope that lies within us'. When the vows we profess become incarnate in our lives, they can become a powerful symbolic force that proclaims Christ to the world. We have seen this in the likes of Vincent de Paul, Thérèse of Lisieux and the Trappists of Tibhirine in Algeria, who were faithful to their vow of stability among their Muslim neighbours unto death.

The way we live the vows, our life of prayer, both private and communal, the way we live community needs to be visible to us within religious life, let alone to those outside it. It needs to have clear, symbolic value and to communicate meaning beyond the routine of a custom and structure that can range from being an unconscious source of support and discipline to being an occupational inconvenience which is endured simply because we have got used to putting up with it. There is room here for considerable originality, freshness and creativity as well as for a more conscious and reflective living of a long tradition. If we believe that religious life has a meaning and a value beyond the merely practical and instrumental, then it is a meaning which must communicate itself to those who live it and those for whose sake it is lived. But perhaps we also need to ask what sort of model of holiness is operative among those who want it all to be so clear, so obvious, so distinctive and different?

The Cambridge theologian Janet Martin Soskice is a Catholic married laywoman who has contributed a trenchant challenge to notions of 'special' or 'distinctive' spiritual criteria in an article entitled 'Love and Attention' in Michael McGhee's *Philosophy, Religion and the Spiritual Life*. In it she discusses the idea, common to writers such as Iris Murdoch, Simone Weil and Charles Taylor, that that which commands our attention and love identifies both who we are and what we should be: 'To be fully human and moral is to respond to that which demands or compels our response – the other attended to with love' (59).

She goes on to discuss the concept in 'received spirituality' of the spiritual person and the spiritual life, which for most of us, she suggests, 'is an eschatological vision – something piously hoped for in the future but far from our daily lives'. The ingredients of such a life in the Catholic tradition would be 'long periods of quiet, focused reflections, dark churches and dignified liturgies […] time spent in contemplative prayer, guided or solitary retreats, and sometimes […] painful wrestlings with God […] above all it involves solitude and collectedness' (61). Soskice contrasts this with the concrete and vexatious banalities of young motherhood, replete as it is with wiping noses, bottoms or anything else leaky, multi-tasking within the household and generally being too exhausted for anything involving seeking God's face. She speaks of the emergence, in the Christian spiritual tradition, of a hierarchy which 'privileges the detached life over […] the demands and turmoils of ordinary domestic life', such a life as generally lived, in classical antiquity, by women, children and slaves. While she concedes that there is a focus in most monastic rules on finding God in simple manual tasks, this is because such tasks leave the mind free to contemplate. 'What we want is a monk who finds God while cooking a meal while one child is clamouring for a drink, another needs a bottom wiped, and a baby throws up over his shoulder'(66). This is certainly far from the serene detachment and passionate concentration on the 'one thing necessary' that is being advocated as the religious ideal by numbers of young adults discerning their vocation who find religious life as currently constituted falling short of their criteria of distinctive excellence.

But God's entry into human history in Jesus baptises, as it were, all human history, so that every aspect of our human life becomes the place where God meets us (71). If that which commands our attention and love identifies both who we are and what we should be, and the particularity of our lives commands God's attention, then there can be no meaningful hierarchy of spiritual value in what is visible of our consecration, and what invisible. All of it becomes the place where God dwells, if we have the eyes to see. The encounter with God is not reserved, then, to the extraordinary, the visible or the distinct in terms of what is different from banal social reality, but in what is precisely most human.

Does this get us off the hook? There is an insight behind the idea that visibility is a good thing, namely, that there has to be something that marks out religious life as a distinct form of life, otherwise there would be no reason for anyone to consider it as a particular form of life, and it would not be one. The problem is that the kind of visibility which focuses upon appearance is not sufficient for a life properly described as religious. The witness of many faithful and effective religious over the past forty years, not to mention the thousands who continued to live religious life in heroic fidelity under the Soviet regime while deprived of all its external trappings, has shown such visibility not to be strictly necessary.[2] If distinctiveness implies that religious life requires or enables one to transcend one's humanity, then such a notion becomes not only questionable but potentially toxic. Visibility as defined merely in terms of external appearance will not wash.

The question remains whether there is an alternative conception of visibility which guarantees that religious life has clear conditions of identity. I believe that the most compelling purpose of and attraction within religious life does not involve our disconnecting from our own self and from humanity but involves the fulfilment of our humanity in the maximal sense. This is not a necessary condition of religious life, since it is clear that you don't have to enter into religious life in order to be human in that normative sense. But then, what would make the religious life option different and worth choosing? The addition of a few visible particularities to an otherwise 'normal' human life cannot make the difference. The survival and flourishing of religious life cannot lie in simply keeping up the appearances and hoping that the reality will look after itself.

Ideally, we would want the visual aspect of religious life to be expressive of the right kind of reality, both for those who live

2. See the DVD 'Interrupted Lives: Catholic Sisters under European Communism' http://www.interruptedlives.org

it and for those who witness it from outside. There are two reasons for thinking that visibility is irrelevant. Firstly when visibility means mere appearance, and secondly when visibility means what is distinctive and what is distinctive gives expression to a problematic conception of humanity, through what is detrimental to humanity (for instance if it is believed that in this way one can avoid the challenge of human sexuality or the drive to possession or power). We have seen all too tragically in recent years what problems such a notion, conscious or unconscious, can lead to.

It came to be thought by many religious, in the aftermath of the council, that many 'visible aspects' of religious life involved divorcing it from the reality it supposedly expressed. For this reason they were abandoned as irrelevant and neither necessary nor sufficient. Visibility in either of these senses had to be rejected. But does it follow that visibility itself has to be rejected? At a time of insecurity and the collapse of self-confidence within any institution it is common to go for one of two options: invisibility or hyper-visibility. Both are problematic. One robs religious life of its powerful symbolic content in a way that can be profoundly disempowering to those who live it and confusing for those who believe in its significance within the church and the world. The other seems to lay claim to a distinctiveness based on a false hierarchy of spiritual value as exclusive as it is dehumanising.

Is it possible instead for us to create a visibility that would give expression to the genuine reality of religious life, embodying who and what we understand ourselves to be and calling others to join us in this particular and distinctive way of being human and Christian? Most thinking adults in search of the common good live out some version of the vows in terms of limiting consumption, pursuing single-hearted and non-instrumental relationships and being willing to live with the good of the community as well as their own personal preferences as a criterion for making choices. But there remain differences, which have, I believe, a major role to play within the church and the world. The symbolic significance of those who embody the religious vows within their own lives remains of crucial importance to the body of Christ.

If religious consecration is to survive it has to be a distinct form of life. If that distinctiveness is to have meaning it must avoid denying what is valuable in human ordinariness and exalting false notions of holiness. If it is to have an impact in the world it must be in dialogue with the crucial signs of our times. Among these I would point to:

- The collapse of a sense of purpose and meaning for human existence
- The fragmentation of family and social relationships
- The scandal of world poverty
- The threat of cosmic ecological disaster
- The loss of an aesthetic value that articulates what is highest in human aspiration.

I believe that religious life can and should visibly embody a hope that challenges the despair and apathy that such losses and threats engender. A life which has risked all for faith can make visible and articulate at both the highest and the most banal domestic levels a deep sense of divine purpose in human living. Our ordinary living and our creative new initiatives within our communities and a wider extended circle can remind us and others of the potential to build powerful and liberating relationships of solidarity beyond the family. The new social media are an extraordinary opportunity for religious to connect with many who long to be supported in their quest for meaning and belonging. For centuries it has been religious communities and individuals who have nurtured what is beautiful in artistic expression of humanity's longing for God. With what energy we have it is worth investing time and resources in creating liturgical prayer and sacred spaces where worship can flourish as an instinctive response and the word of God can echo deep within peoples' lives. 2010 saw a ban on fishing in the Sea of Galilee because of the critical depletion of stocks. As a symbol of the crisis that greed and heedlessness have brought upon our world it could barely be starker. The values embodied in vows of poverty, chastity and obedience surely offer a powerful symbolic response to the ecological crisis: acting justly and sustainably, loving tenderly and in human solidarity, walking humbly with God as we listen attentively to where the Spirit is leading us through the signs of the times.

Recently I received a bizarre request from a television company to appear in a show where they wanted me to line up with some actresses from *Sister Act* while competitors guessed which one of us was the real nun. I was assured that the spectacle would be 'totally respectful' and was offered, by way of enticement, a donation to my favourite charity. Apart from the fact that the competitors would have had to be blind and brain dead not to notice the glaring differences between my physique and that of a professional dancer, I wondered how they would have judged the matter. The cultural and ideological battles which took up so much time and energy among religious in the immediate aftermath of the council are over. If religious life is to have a future, we need *ressourcement* as well as *aggiornamento*, a look at the origins and purpose of our life as gifted by the Spirit to and mandated by the church. If the visibility of our life is not necessarily one that would be obvious in an identity parade, I do believe that it is time we visited again the whole question of the distinctiveness and particularity of a life which continues, despite our many frailties, to have a beauty and a significance beyond the sum of individuals who are called to it.

Reflection questions
1. What do you understand by the visibility or particularity of religious life?
2. How do you and your congregation make this clear to the world?
3. If you were to revisit this question, what changes might you make?

9

Religious Life Looks to its Future

James Sweeney CP

Introduction

Discussion of the current trajectory of religious life and its future prospects often makes reference to the successive emergence of new forms of this way of life across the centuries. The schema is well known: the desert period; the age of the monasteries; the mendicant orders founded in medieval times; the sixteenth-century apostolic orders; the nineteenth-century congregations mainly devoted to teaching, health and social care and missions; and the early to mid-twentieth-century new groups such as the secular institutes. The question naturally arises, in the context of the dislocations that have occurred since the mid-1960s as well as the rise of the 'new movements', as to where religious life is now heading, and whether some new global form or paradigm of religious life is developing? Against this background, this chapter reflects on the prospects for the future of religious life.

One can identify at least three distinct paradigms in the historical record: the eremitical, the monastic (incorporating monastic and mendicant), and the apostolic (beginning in the sixteenth century with the Jesuits and the Ursulines and continuing to the present day). The apostolic religious life is the form specific to modernity, spanning modernity's earliest inception at the time of the Reformation through to the present 'post-modern' times. All previous forms are born out of antiquity and the medieval world. Of course, the historical forms of one era continue into succeeding eras; the history is one of accumulation rather than displacement. The witness of each era is maintained in the following eras, while it is also modified by the new circumstances; the process is one of mutual enrichment.

The essential argument pursued here is, firstly, that there is indeed a need today for some fundamental re-articulation of religious life, whether or not that implies a radically new paradigm; and secondly, that while some stabilisation of religious life is now discernable in at least some of the monastic-mendicant inspired orders, for religious life to be fully fit for the future depends ultimately on a renewal within the apostolic paradigm. This thesis requires a much fuller historical and theoretical enquiry than can be provided here; all that will be attempted is to lay out the bare bones of the argument with some limited examples and references.

Religious Life 'paradigms', church 'formations' and social change
The historical religious life paradigms are closely related to what Staf Hellemans calls 'church formations'. In his definition: 'The concept of "church formation" refers to a historical constellation – with a number of basic structural characteristics – typical for a church in a particular period of time.'[1] These structural features are, in turn, related to the social and cultural circumstances of the epochs in which the church formation emerges, and one of the main triggers of a formation or paradigm shift is a transformation in the wider society. A church formation derives not simply from church policy. Popes and councils may discern the kind of formation needed, but it itself is the fruit of a complex historical process.

Lessons from History
Concentrating on the modern era, and without going into all the long history, it is evident that the religious life, the church and the society of the nineteenth century were all markedly different from the eighteenth. The great events which inaugurated modernity in its full sense around the turn of the nineteenth century – the French Revolution, the demise of the *ancien régime*, the Enlightenment, the industrial revolution – were also influential in the immense ecclesiastical changes of that period, first in a negative way but then more positively. The church was, of course, active and not simply passive in the face of these social changes and influential in shaping the emerging order, and re-shaping itself in the process. This is clear both from the sixteenth century counter-Reformation as well as the nineteenth century changes. Church leadership responded vigorously to the

---

1. Staf Hellemans, 'A Critical Transition: From Ultramontane Mass Catholicism to Choice Catholicism', in P.C. Beentjes (ed.) *The Catholic Church and Modernity in Europe*, (Tilburg Theological Studies, Berlin: LIT Verlag, 2009), pp. 32-54.

dramatic challenges of these times, and with remarkable success. With post-Tridentine Catholicism a definitively new church formation in contrast to the medieval church came into being (seminaries, the catechism, re-organisation of dioceses). And there was a marked, if perhaps less dramatic, re-shaping of Catholicism between the eighteenth-century church of Clement XIV (1769-74) and Pius VI (1775-99) and the nineteenth-century 'ultramontane' church of Pius IX (1846-78) and Leo XIII (1878-1903).

In the eighteenth century, the Catholic Church was still a largely devolved body, with dioceses and local church provinces exercising almost complete control over their own affairs (the appointment of bishops, for example), although under strong state influence, but the nineteenth century saw a centralisation and greater direct governance by the papacy. Religious life also went through a major transition. There was a dramatic drop in numbers between the end of the eighteenth and the early nineteenth centuries, due to disbandment of the Jesuits (1773) and confiscation of church property by governments and the wholesale suppression of the monasteries across much of Europe. The number of religious built up again from the late nineteenth century, reaching unprecedented heights by the mid-twentieth century.

The main feature of Catholicism in the later nineteenth century, according to Hellemans, was mass mobilisation. The Catholic people of Europe were re-organised to resist the secular, anti-religious culture and to re-fashion a Christian conception of society. This church formation was centred on the papacy – it was 'ultra-montane' – and Pope Leo XIII installed Thomist philosophy as its intellectual underpinnings, while the tradition of Catholic social teaching begun by his encyclical *Rerum Novarum* (1891) gave it its social programme. The resurgence of religious life at this time led to many new foundations to meet the new educational and social needs and a new missionary drive to take the gospel to the territories the European powers were colonising.

Contemporary Challenges
What, then, about today? For half a century and more we have been living through a massive societal transformation, leading

to what cultural theorists call 'post-modernity' and more cautious sociologists see as 'late modernity' or 'high' or 'advanced' modernity. This change gives credence to the thesis of an emerging new church formation postulated by Hellemans as a shift from 'ultramontane mass Catholicism' to 'choice Catholicism' – within which an incipient paradigm shift in religious life may also be under way. How important is today's social transformation? It is clearly global in scope, evident from the phenomenon of globalisation, the financial crisis of 2008, the collapse of the Soviet Union and the communist system, global warming and droughts and famines and flooding. Few would question the extent or depth of the challenge of the future, and to the future of humanity as a whole.[2] There are many ways of analysing the nature of this change in late modernity. Here we will explore just one issue, significant for the topic in hand: individualisation and its theological and spiritual implications.

Today's social transformation impacts across the whole range of our social institutions: politics, trade unions, education, churches and faith traditions, and it also questions institutional-isation itself. Nineteenth century modernity was the great era of institutions. Western society was put on a new bureaucratically organised basis: 'Who says modernity says not just organisations but organisation', says Anthony Giddens, and the far-reaching organisational re-development of the church was fit for those times.[3] But today our institutions are questioned; they no longer have the solid security they enjoyed in classical modernity. Industrialisation delivered 'jobs for life', something today's high-tech society does away with. Personal identification and loyalty to the organisation which could once be presumed now has to be won, and it is always fragile.

The post-modern individual is suspicious of institutions and is preoccupied more with the self. We seek fulfilment in personal experience over commitment to a cause, whether a political cause, a marriage, a job, a vocation. This is more than simple

---

2. See Nicholas Boyle, 2014: *How to Survive the Next World Crisis*, (London: Continuum, 2010).
3. Anthony Giddens, *Modernity and Self-Identity: Self and Society in the Late Modern Age*, (Cambridge: Polity Press, 1991), p. 16.

narcissism, even if that is not lacking. The underlying shift is in the relation of the individual to the social order; there is a deepening individualisation. This is central to today's societal transformation, and it fits with the idea of 'choice Catholicism'.

Individualisation should not be confused with simple individualism. Of course the much vaunted valuing of the individual is full of ambiguities. Thought of as standing free from control and with a new capacity for choice, the individual is yet subject to masked controls and constraints; hidden persuaders operate in a consumer society; the 'brave new' individual is as much burdened by choice as empowered by it. And yet, in an ever more complex, specialist, high-tech, knowledge-based society, where individuals can only be 'a part' and never 'the whole', it is only by a greater cultural stress on individuality that they can assert themselves as more than a mere cog in the machine. The assertion of the self is a social necessity given the nature of contemporary society. The specialist skills needed, not only for working but simply for living today favour a more individualised self. With the shift to the self the value of personal experience becomes prominent; lived experience exercises a fascination and takes on a significance that is quite different from previous times – a change that is captured in the adage 'from the experience of authority to the authority of experience'.

Individualisation raises profound social, cultural, moral, spiritual and institutional questions. Can the 'assertion of the self' be reconciled with the gospel injunction to 'abandon oneself'? It all depends on the kind of assertion and abandonment in question. The cultural 'spirituality' which is much in vogue today majors on the theme of the self, and at many points it is at odds with Christian spirituality. However, there can be convergence as well as divergence, for social reality does not simply collide with evangelical injunction; it also contains 'signs of the times' awaiting evangelical scrutiny. The theme of individualisation is central to the social and cultural make-up of late modernity; in fact, the argument here is that it is the key feature. Will the next church formation, then, be 'choice Catholicism'? The proposal has evident sociological credibility; it is in tune with today's looser institutional claims on the individual. On the other hand, Catholicism always puts a premium on the communal, and this seems to be underplayed by the emphasis on choice, even though it is clear that nineteenth-century style mass mobilisation could not succeed today.

The main theological proposal put forward today is the model of *communio*. *Communio* ecclesiology has been one of the most promising post-conciliar developments and it has been the key to opening up many blockages, both internally in the church and ecumenically. The *communio* model re-focuses the purpose of the institutional church in service of relationship – relationships between human persons, and that relationship of life in the Trinity which is the ultimate mystery of Christian existence as drawn into the intimate life of Father, Son and Holy Spirit. This ecclesiology integrates the communal and individual in a personalist philosophy: the communal is understood as serving the good of the person, while the individual is understood as 'person-in-community'. Has the *communio* model the potential to open up a new church formation for the twenty-first century? Might the transition be re-expressed in a theological-normative way as 'from Conformist Catholicism to *Communio* Catholicism'? This would integrate personal choice and individualisation with the communal. However, a latent stress on the communal over against, or instead of, the individual could be read into the notion of *communio*. And, as is well known, *communio* is some-times only an empty rhetoric, a cover for insisting on conformity.

These are the issues of the day; they await resolution in the course of historical change. Their repercussions for religious life are profound, and religious life is itself involved in working them through. The orders are faced with the concurrent issue of their own. What paradigm of religious life is required for the future?

Religious Life – Contemporary Dynamics
As the twenty-first century enters its second decade the enthusiasm for renewal inspired by the Second Vatican Council is a distant dream and the troubles that have bedevilled religious life, including but not confined to its major post-1960s numerical decline, show little sign of abating. The anxiety expressed by Pope John Paul II about the risk of a disastrous loss of confidence in its very validity as an ecclesial way of life remains prescient:

'What must be avoided at all costs is the actual breakdown of the consecrated life, a collapse which is not measured by a decrease in numbers but by a failure to cling steadfastly to the Lord and to personal vocation and mission' (*Vita consecrata*, 63).

With Vatican II, the Catholic Church took a new view of the modern world, and it seemed to abandon its previous rejectionist stance. John XXIII's vision was that the church had weathered the storms of modernity and come through rather well, and was in a position to make a new kind of contribution to society and help to secure its value base. The Catholicism of the early 1960s did not feel under pressure from hostile social forces; and where it was, as in the case of communism, it felt confident enough to face the challenges openly and even sympathetically. Only the conservatives at the council – Pope John's 'prophets of doom' – disagreed, and they were vanquished in the debates. A new 'church formation' seemed to be emerging, with *Gaudium et spes* as its charter.

As the post-conciliar era developed, however, there was a shift back to a stance of confrontation with the world, with the present times eventually seen emblematically as a 'culture of death'. It would be an exaggeration to see this as a total *volte face*, and it was certainly justified to take a more critical view of the trends that emerged from the late 1960s onwards. But the new caution among the church leadership threw in doubt the extent to which a new church formation would be embraced, and it also de-legitimised many of the responses to the council that had taken hold in religious life.

What, then, have been the results of the past half century effort of renewal in the Catholic Church? Without going into the many details, or drawing up a balance sheet of successes and failures, we can note the two contrary tendencies that are now seen to be in competition over the future – renewal or restoration ('full steam ahead' or 'back to the future'). In religious life these tendencies take flesh as different models which, for the purposes of description, we can call the 'prophetic' and the 'observant'. This rough and ready distinction is worth sketching out in detail, fleshing the two models out as 'ideal types' in the sociological sense. Ideal types accentuate certain characteristics as typical features, but they should not be confused with concrete descriptions. There are a range of ways in which the ideal types may be realised in practice.

Prophetic versus Observant

The prophetic model relies on a theology of the kingdom of God, a lifestyle of open engagement with the world and its needs, promoting justice and peace; it is similar in form to a 'social movement', a flexible 'current' within the church and society. Religious life lived this way can be seen as a modest service, not fixated on having to come up with final 'solutions' to today's problems and challenges, but responding to human and pastoral needs in small but symbolic ways, with fresh and creative forms of witness, and sustaining hope for humanity's future. The 'observant' model, by contrast, emphasises the received structural forms of religious life, community life and monastic-style practices; mission is framed in terms of evangelisation, and ministries give pride of place to prayer and spirituality.[4]

The prophetic model may mean a small religious community inserted into a poor area, living in a council house and responding to local needs as they arise; or a community in charge of a parish promoting fair trade; or running a school and putting the emphasis on education for justice. The observant model may mean traditional style monastic observance (even, sometimes, adhering to the 'Extraordinary Rite'); or running a parish or a spirituality centre with an emphasis on evangelisation and charismatic prayer, perhaps using the Alpha course.

The prophetic model rose to prominence in the years after Vatican II and was more or less captured in many orders' revised constitutions. But it quickly ran into difficulties, at least in the west. Its trajectory has been similar in many ways to that of liberation theology, which is one of its sources of inspiration. The 'prophetics' became entangled in the many difficulties and controversies of the post-conciliar era: the departures from religious life, the drop in vocations, the closure of institutions. In fact, the 'prophetic opening' could easily be blamed for these troubles by departing from the well-tried ways of the past. But

---

4. See James Sweeney, 'Prophets & Parables: A Future for Religious Orders', Informationes Theologiae Europae, Göttingen (August 2001), pp. 273-292.

the really difficult entanglement for the 'prophetics' was not a conflict with the conservative or more observantly oriented forces but, more damagingly, that they were caught up in conflict with some regressive tendencies that emerged in the wake of the council both in the church at large and internally in religious life. To continue with the individualisation theme, a slide into individualism in reaction to the conformism of the pre-conciliar era was all too easy, with a consequent withdrawal from communal responsibility. This de-stabilised many communities and foiled attempts at renewal. Meanwhile, the pioneers of new ways: moving into new social ministries, founding 'communities of insertion', etc, could be tarred with the same brush of 'doing their own thing' (and maybe sometimes not without reason).

In contrast to these post-conciliar confusions, the new orders and movements made their appearance as a fresh beginning. They eschew polarised controversies, and restore well understood traditional themes and practices (e.g. eucharistic adoration, the religious habit), while marrying them to the modern impulses of option for the poor, simplicity of life, spirituality. And there is a seeming knock-down argument in their favour - whatever vocations are going seem to go to them! However, they now seem to be going through a period of testing. Sociologists tell of the 'routinisation of charisma', the phase which typically follows that of the founder. It is a troubling time when the life force of charisma is tested, when the special appeal of the founder and the enthusiasm of the beginnings fade. Will the enterprise endure? All the indications are that the 'new movements' are now entering this phase. Some are in crisis, some of the founders have died, others have been found wanting.

We should not over-emphasise the differences between these two models of religious life; there is much common ground between them: simplicity of lifestyle, involvement with the poor, a contemplative spirit. The observant life carefully followed by monks and nuns is prophetic. The prophetic lifestyle of the 'inserted community' is observant of a defined rule of life. Nevertheless, there is a difference in tone, and most religious will know instinctively which model they identify with in the round.

The Trajectory of Change

In attempting to assess these diverse post-conciliar experiences in the perspective of the evolution of religious life paradigms, a first observation is that the success of the new movements derives both from their own undoubted charismatic provenance, evident, for example, in strong leaders, communal energy, charismatic renewal style of spirituality, and their adoption, for the most part, of structures and practices associated with the monastic-mendicant form. Moreover, the established monastic-mendicant orders seem, in general, to have weathered the post-conciliar/post-modern storms better than the apostolic orders. Monastic life is a ready response to the contemporary search for community and spirituality. Monasteries are places of retreat, and they can be the base for new forms of lay community. This suggests that the trajectory of future change will continue to draw deeply from this particular font in the historical patrimony.

The puzzle is the difficulties the apostolic orders have faced. Why has the form of charisma that emerged among them: in search of the kingdom of God, engaging directly with the conditions and life struggles of people today, committing to justice and social transformation, living and serving among the poor, why has this apparently failed to become a self-sustaining movement? Why has it attracted relatively few recruits?

The direction of change in the apostolic orders after the council, in their new forms of community and general lifestyle and established works, was more secular in tone than what prevailed among the new movements. Explicit religious structures such as devotions, the religious habit, traditional ministries, and even emphasis on the religious vows and rule, were superseded by a new impulse of engagement, especially in the option for the poor, a move from the traditional *fuga mundi* to *Gaudium et spes*.

There are those who maintain that this change was quite simply a mistake; that loosening the tension with 'the world' only resulted in a loss of religious visibility and, more devastatingly, in a disastrous loss of motivation for religious living. There is no doubt, as already stated, that renewal was compromised by some negative influences. But there was a sense of religious life being called by the council to something really new. A radical sense of newness was in the air, but it was ill-defined, and therefore difficult to grasp. By contrast, the new movements' stress on continuity, and traditional and less 'worldly' values such as eucharistic adoration, Marian devotion, loyalty to the papacy, etc, were quite specific.

There were institutional constraints placed by church authority on some of the developments in apostolic religious life (eg. the troubled relationship between the Jesuits and the Vatican). This was similar to the institutional disapproval of liberation theology. A 'political' analysis of these dynamics could help explain the limited success of the prophetic model. However, religious orders have always come up against institutional obstacles, and one indication of authenticity is their capacity eventually to surmount them.

If the shift towards 'the ordinary' from the 'the religious' has been problematic, it is nevertheless coherent with the founding inspiration of many apostolic religious congregations, particularly institutes of women religious and those established in the nineteenth century. And, as Charles Taylor shows in his ground-breaking analysis of the emergence of the modern world, the embrace of 'the ordinary' is a central theme.[6] It would be facile, therefore, to dismiss the contemporary experience of the apostolic orders as of little account, however difficult it has been.

What it does suggest, however, is the need to explore the nature of the fundamental impulse of the apostolic religious life. Vatican II directed the orders to return *ad fontes*, to their origins, in order to rediscover their founding charism. What, then, is the origin, source and the character of the gift received from the Spirit which constitutes the charism of the apostolic orders and gives them their ecclesial identity?

Charism

Religious life, in all of its diversity and manifestations, derives from and exhibits a special fascination with the person of Jesus Christ. This gives it its fundamental character as *sequela Christi*. It is a particular following of Christ, a path marked out within the baptismal calling. In this sense, the religious life is also called

---

6. See Charles Taylor, *Sources of the Self*, (Cambridge: Cambridge University Press, 1991) and *A Secular Age*, (Cambridge MA: Harvard University Press, 2007).

'consecrated life', a renewed consecration within baptismal consecration.[7] The classic understanding of a religious institute, and one that is attested in the lives of founders, is that it is not the result of a simple human decision to create a new organisation but is 'the work of God', understood in a strong sense. A religious institute understands itself (or so the founders understand it) as an ongoing work, a re-occurring event. It is a participation in the divine mystery, with historical origins in the life and experience of the founder. The charism, the gift of the Spirit, is given to the founder and is transmitted, while also re-expressed, in the life and experience of subsequent generations. A charism is marked by history; by the history of the times in which it arises and the time-bound needs which it answers, and also by the history of its reception in the founded community and the response it generates.

Charism is an impulse that is interiorly felt, a spiritual experience, and also a call to serve. Within the eremitical paradigm and that of classical monasticism the Spirit inspires the search for a more total Christian commitment (*fuga mundi*, common life). In the mendicant, and even more in the apostolic orders, charism is more focused. Francis's profound spiritual experience includes a call to 'rebuild my church'; Dominic is called to preach and counter heresy. With Ignatius, his spiritual experience is clearly foundational; the elements of his *Spiritual Exercises* resonate first of all in his personal biography. Something of modernity's turn to the self becomes evident here. There is an enhanced emphasis on the founder's personal spiritual experience and personal history, and this is deeply implicated in the shape the charism takes. Finally, these 'events of the Spirit' in the diverse apostolic orders focus on some particular facet of the gospel, some dimension of the person and redeeming work of Christ, the *mysterium fidei*. Out of this inspiration orders derive their *raison d'être* and apostolic purpose.

Charism is a matter of pneumatology, of the theology of Holy Spirit, and the religious life in the church belongs to its charismatic rather than institutional dimension, the dimension

---

7. See James Sweeney, 'Consecrated Life: The Synod and Theology', *Religious Life Review,* Vol 35 (March-April 1995) pp. 75-85.

of its Spirit inspired life and holiness. Popes and bishops do not, or do not normally, establish religious orders. Their role as institutional guardians is to receive and recognise the work of the Spirit in the founders. This is the paradox of the canonical regulation of religious life - an example of the institutionalisation of charisma.

The Apostolic Paradigm

The Spirit 'blows where it wills', and at crucial historical junctures directs the church in new paths. The apostolic religious life properly so called came into being in the sixteenth century with the challenges of the Reformation and the new world of early modernity. It was a further development of the mission the mendicant orders had already undertaken when they opened up traditional monasticism and equipped it for the task of carrying the gospel into the changing society of the thirteenth century. There was, however, a difference.

The burning theological question in the sixteenth century was where and how God is to be found. Is God to be found in the church, in its authority and teachings and sacramental practices? Or in the personal faith of believers, their reading of the scriptures and a life lived according to its teachings as interpreted by conscience? Is God to be found in the church or the world, through a life in community or through a life lived out in the world? The western church split over such issues, although the split was never a really clean one in terms of a stark choice between the two approaches. It was in this context that the apostolic paradigm of religious life first began to take shape.

The dynamic of the apostolic charism is the call to a work in the world. It is primarily a mission, and from this flows a community and a sense of identity. The foundational spiritual experience bears these marks – the *sequela Christi* as a call to ministerial service, the acceptance of a mission, the gathering of companions, and the emergence of a new path of Christian discipleship. This is clear in the instance of the Jesuits, for whom mission in the world took priority over communal living. In subsequent centuries many new religious orders took the same direction, although they articulated this apostolic paradigm in different ways. Founders are eclectic; they draw on the panoply of spiritual and institutional resources of the whole historic religious life tradition, on 'things ancient and new'.

However, many of these orders had great difficulty in gaining ecclesiastical approval for their particular proposals. This was especially true of orders of women which were put under pressure, even into the late nineteenth century, to adopt monastic enclosure. Today many of these orders, in response to the council's mandate to return *ad fontes*, have re-visited the historical conflicts of their origins and sought to recapture their founding inspiration. But even now this apostolic religious life charisma is a difficult 'fit' with the predominant patterns of the institutional church. It was ever so.[8]

Conclusion: the End of the Beginning?
If the analysis presented here has credibility, then the surprise previously alluded to about the apostolic orders' difficulties with renewal is not so surprising after all. It is what could be expected. Such 'success' as there has been in renewing religious life has been within the monastic-mendicant paradigm. More problematic have been the changes initiated among the apostolic orders, which have strayed beyond the accepted paradigm. But any radical departures, a new paradigm, or in this case the re-articulation of the apostolic paradigm, will necessarily be fraught with difficulty and will be contested. But is some form of paradigm change really needed; is it a realistic prospect? There is no need to imagine some totally new future for religious life, but there are socio-cultural and theological arguments in favour of a paradigm shift. In the first place, there is the argument that the critical challenge of post-modernity is the challenge of meaning more than the challenge of community. In other words, the contemporary search for community, a genuine search to which monastic life responds very well, does not get to the absolute heart of the matter. A sense of communal belonging supports but does not fully address or resolve the challenges of individualisation. Issues of the self are involved which raise deeper existential questions of meaning. In Grace Davie's terms,

---

8. The twelfth-century Franciscan movement was at risk of splitting from the institutional Church — one reason, it is said, for the speedy canonisation of Francis.

the religious identity of most people today is a matter of 'believing without belonging'.[9] Even as we become free-floating individuals without a religious community (or indeed with one) we still desperately need to find what to believe in. It is the fate of the post-modern individual.

The theological argument for paradigm shift is about the question of how God is to be found; this is as live an issue today as it was in the sixteenth century, and it has been given a new twist with the theology of the option for the poor. If the primordial place of God's presence is among his people, and in a special way among the poor, and if, arguably, this incarnational approach is the fundamental orientation of the church today, then one would expect to find it strongly reflected, both spiritually and ministerially, in the contemporary religious life paradigm.

These are not knock-down arguments, merely suggestive of some determinants of the future, what course religious life might chart between *communio* and choice, the prophetic and the observant. Of course, this is but one reading of the situation, and I readily grant that alternative interpretations can be put on the historical prospects. Where, then, does it all leave the project of renewal? In the church at large, renewal as understood by the council seems largely to have stalled. A policy of resistance to institutional change, stressing historic continuities and rehabilitating traditional practices, has been adopted. We have now moved beyond the ecclesial era of Vatican II; the post-conciliar period is at an end. This does not mean any simple return to the pre-Vatican II church, but the powerful impulse that erupted at Vatican II and reverberated throughout the church, and which was taken with complete seriousness by religious communities, has subsided. Reference may still be made to the documents of the council but the dynamism it sparked has faded.

But the question remains: what now? What of religious life? The Spirit continues to 'blow where it wills'. And the charismatic impulse has its own rhythms. As the 'new movements' confront the unfamiliar challenges of routinisation, and as the mood among the established apostolic orders after all their efforts at

9. Grace Davie, *Religion in Britain since 1945: Believing Without Belonging*, (London, Blackwell, 1994).

renewal is one of puzzled inertia, the forces both of renewal and of restoration are at a crisis point. This must surely energise the debate and even a daring willingness to seize the future.

It may mean that renewal is now at the end of the beginning.

Reflection questions
1. The author describes a shift from 'ultramontane mass Catholicism' to 'choice Catholicism' within which a paradigm shift in religious life may also be under way. What are the characteristics of this shift, and how have they affected religious life?
2. Does your congregation belong to the 'prophetic' or the 'observant' model as described here? What do you see as the advantages or disadvantages of this?
3. What might religious life have to say today to a generation whose religious identity is a matter of 'believing without belonging'?

Bibliography

Arbuckle, Gerald A., *Culture, Inculturation and Theologians: a Postmodern Critique*, (Collegeville, Liturgical Press, 2010)

Barth, Karl, *Dogmatics in Outline*, (London, SCM, 1966)

Beattie, Tina, *New Catholic Feminism: Theology and Theory*, (London, Routledge, 2006)

Beentjes, P.C. (ed), *The Catholic Church and Modernity in Europe*, (Tilburg Theological Studies,Vol 3, Berlin: LIT Verlag, 2010)

St Benedict, *The Rule of St Benedict*, (Stanbrook Abbey, 1937)

Benedict XVI, 'Pastoral Letter to the Catholics of Ireland', 4, March 2010, http://www.vatican.va/holy_father/benedict_xvi/letters/2010/documents/hf_ben-xvi_let_20100319_church-ireland_en.html

—, 'Christmas Greetings to Curia', December 2005 [http://www.vatican.va/holy_father/benedict_xvi/speeches/2005/december/documents/hf_ben_xvi_spe_20051222_roman-curia_en.html

—, 'Address to Superiors General of the Institutes of Consecrated Life and Societies of Apostolic Life', 10, May 22, 2006 http://www.vatican.va/holy_father/benedict_xvi/speeches/2006/may/documents/hf_ben-xvi_spe_20060522_vita-consacrata_en.html

—, *Deus Caritas Est*

Bendyna, Mary E. and Mary L. Gautier, *Recent Vocations to Religious Life: a Report for the National Religious Vocation Conference*, 2009

Breton, Stanislaus, *The Passionist Congregation and Its Charism: Studies in Passionist History and Spirituality*, (Rome, Passionist Generalate 1987)

Bouyer, Louis, *The Paschal Mystery*, (London, George Allen & Unwin, 1951)

Boyle, Nicholas, 2014: *How to Survive the Next World Crisis*, (London: Continuum, 2010)

Brink, Laurie, 'A Marginal Life: Pursuing Holiness in the Twenty-First Century', *Horizon*, Spring 2008

Bulgakov, Sergei, *Sophia: The Wisdom of God*, (Hudson, Lindis-farne Press, 1993)

Burrell, David B., *Knowing the Unknowable God: Ibn-Sina, Maimonides, Aquinas* (Notre Dame: University of Notre Dame Press, 1986)

Butler, Sarah, 'Apostolic Religious Life: a Public, Ecclesial Vocation' September 2008
http://www.stonehill.edu/x14963.xml

Cada, Laurence, *et al, Shaping the Coming Age of Religious Life*, (New York, Seabury Press, 1979)

Chávez Villanueva, Pascual, 'The Word of God and Salesian Life Today', *Acts of the General Council of the Salesian Society of St John Bosco*, July-September 2004

Cardman, Francine, 'Vatican II Revisited', *America*, 4-11 January 2010

Chittister, Joan, *The Fire In These Ashes: a Spirituality of Contemporary Religious Life*, (London, Sheed & Ward, 1995)

Clifford, Anne M., *Introducing Feminist Theology*, (New York, Orbis, 2001)

Coakley, Sarah, *Powers and Submissions: Spirituality, Philosophy and Gender*, (Oxford, Blackwell, 2002)

Coffey, Mary Finbarr, (unpublished PhD thesis, Heythrop College, University of London, 2010)

Congregation for Institutes of Consecrated Life and Societies of Apostolic Life, *Starting Afresh from Christ: a Renewed Commitment to Consecrated Life in the Third Millennium*, 2002

Council of Major Superiors of Women Religious (ed), *The Foundations of Religious Life: Revisiting the Vision*, (Notre Dame, Ave Maria, 2009)

Cunningham, Michael, *Let Your Heart Pray: Spirituality for Contemplatives in Action* (Bolton: Don Bosco Publications, 2009)
"Few Words and a Lot of Action ...": an Introduction to the Working Style of Don Bosco Youth, Net ivzw (Heverleee: Don Bosco Youth-Net ivzw, no date), http://www.donboscoyouth.net/system/files/Few+words+and+a+lot+of+action.pdf

Davie, Grace, *Religion in Britain since 1945: Believing without Belonging*, (London, Blackwell, 1994)

Flannery, Austen (ed), *Vatican Council II: The Conciliar and Post Conciliar Documents*, (Dublin, Dominican Publications, 1992)

Giddens, Anthony, *Modernity and Self-Identity: Self and Society in the Late Modern Age*, (Cambridge: Polity Press, 1991)

Groeschel, Benedict, *A Drama of Reform*, (San Francisco, Ignatius Press, 2005)

Hampson, Daphne, *Theology and Feminism*, (Oxford, Blackwell, 1990)

—, (ed), *Swallowing a Fishbone? Feminist Theologians Debate Christianity*, (London, SPCK, 1996)

Hanvey, James, 'Refounding: Living in the Middle Time,' in *The Way Supplement* 101 (2001), *Refounding: Church and Spirituality*

Henggeler, Rudolf, *Das Institut der Lehrschwestern vom Heiligen Kreuz in Menzingen* (Kt Zug), (Menzingen, 1944)

Iona Institute, *Marriage Breakdown and Family Structure in Ireland*, 2007

Jones, L. (ed), *Encyclopaedia of Religion*, (London, Macmillan, 2005)

Keen, Andrew, *The Cult of the Amateur: How Today's Internet Is Killing Our Culture and Assaulting Our Economy*, (Nicholas Brealey, 2007)

Ker, Ian, *The New Movements: a Theological Introduction*, (CTS, 2001)

King, Ursula, *Women and Spirituality: Voices of Protest and Promise*, (London, MacMillan, 1989)

Livingstone, E.A. (ed), *The Oxford Dictionary of the Christian Church*, (Oxford, Oxford University Press, 1997)

McGhee, Michael (ed), *Philosophy, Religion and the Spiritual Life*, (Cambridge, Cambridge University Press, 1992)

Mackenzie, Catriona, and Natalie Stoljar (eds), *Relational Autonomy: Feminist Perspectives on Autonomy, Agency and the Social Self*, (Oxford, Oxford University Press, 2000)

Mannion, Gerard (ed), *The Vision of John Paul II: Assessing His Thought and Influence*, (Collegeville, Liturgical Press, 2008)

Mowry LaCugna, Catherine (ed), *Freeing Theology: the Essentials of Theology in Feminist Perspective* (New York, Harper Collins, 1993)

Murray, Paul, 'The Need for an Integrated Theology of Ministry within Contemporary Catholicism', *Concilium* 2010/1

O'Connell, Andrew, 'Vocation Ministry in Ireland Today' in *Horizon*, Spring 2009

O'Grady, Colm (ed), *The Challenge to Religious Life Today*, (London, Chapman, 1970)

Ó Murchú, Diarmuid, *Reframing Religious Life*, (London, St Paul's, 1998)

Parenti, S. *et al* (eds), *Evlogema: Studies in Honour of Robert Taft SJ*, (Rome, Studia Anselmiana, 1993)

Rodé, Cardinal Franc, 'Reforming Religious Life with the Right Hermeneutic', 4-5, September 2008
http://www.stonehill.edu/x14963.xml

Pontifical Council for Culture & Pontifical Council for Interreligious Dialogue, *Jesus Christ - The Bearer of the Water of Life*, 2003

Radcliffe, Timothy, *I Call You Friends*, (London, Continuum), 2001

—, *Why Go to Church? The Drama of the Eucharist* (London: Continuum, 2008)

Radford Ruether, Rosemary, *Sexism and God-Talk: Towards a Feminist Theology*, (London, SCM, 1983)

Rainer Peters, Tiemo, and Claus Urban, *Ende der Zeit? Die Provokation der Rede von Gott* (Mainz, Matthias-Grünewald-Verlag 1999)

Schillebeeckx, Edward, *Interim Report on the Books Jesus and Christ*, (London: SCM Press, 1980)

—, *God Among Us: the Gospel Proclaimed*, (London: SCM Press, 1983)

—, *Jesus in Our Western Culture: Mysticism, Ethics and Politics*, (London: SCM Press, 1987)

—, *Church: the Human Story of God*, (London: SCM Press, 1990)

Schneiders, Sandra M., *Finding the Treasure*, (New York, Paulist Press, 2000)

—, *Selling All*, (New York, Paulist Press, 2001)

—, *Beyond Patching: Faith and Feminism in the Catholic Church*, (revised edition, New York, Paulist Press, 2004)

—, 'Why we Stay(ed)', *Concilium* 2010/1

Schüssler Fiorenza, Elisabeth, *Discipleship of Equals: A Critical Feminist Ekklesialogy of Liberation*, (New York Crossroad, 1993)

Slee, Nicola, *The Book of Mary*, (London, SPCK, 2007)

Speed Thompson, Daniel, *The Language of Dissent: Edward Schillebeeckx on the Crisis of Authority in the Catholic Church*, (Notre Dame, University of Notre Dame Press, 2003)

Spidlik, S., *The Spirituality of the Christian East*, (Kalamazoo, 1986)

Stogdon, Katharine M., 'The Risk of Surrender: Se Livrer in the Life of Thérèse Couderc (1805-1885)', Ph.D. thesis, University of Manchester, 2004.

Sweeney, James, 'Consecrated Life: The Synod and Theology', *Religious Life Review*, Vol 35 (March-April 1995)

—, 'Prophets & Parables: A Future for Religious Orders', *Informationes Theologiae Europae*, Gottingen (August 2001)

—, *et al* (general eds), *Going Forth: an Enquiry into Evangelization and Renewal in the Roman Catholic Church in England & Wales. Research Report*, (Cambridge, Von Hügel Institute and Margaret Beaufort Institute of Theology), November 2006

—, with Gemma Simmonds & David Lonsdale (eds), *Keeping Faith in Practice: Aspects of Catholic Pastoral Theology*, (London: SCM, 2010)

Tanner, Kathryn, *God and Creation in Christian Theology: Tyranny or Empowerment?* (Oxford: Blackwell, 1988)

Taylor, Charles, *The Sources of the Self*, (Cambridge: CUP, 1991)

—, *A Secular Age*, (Cambridge MA: Harvard University Press, 2007)

Vanhoozer, Kevin (ed), *The Cambridge Companion to Postmodern Theology*, (Cambridge, Cambridge University Press, 2003)

Von Speyr, Adrienne, *Handmaid of the Lord*, (San Francisco, Ignatius Press, 1985)

Waters, John, *Lapsed Agnostic*, (London, Continuum, 2008)

Wittberg, Patricia, *From Piety to Professionalism--and Back?: Transformations of Organized Religious Virtuosity*, (Lanham, Lexington Books, 2006)